"A must-read for all those in the Campbell movement who have long desired to welcome the Spirit back into the churches"

"Postmoderns yearn for genuine spirituality. Are Churches of Christ prepared to respond to this cultural search? Allen and Swick believe there are resources within our heritage to meet this need, but it was a road we failed to take. They recall a missed opportunity in the 1850s and call contemporary Churches of Christ to reconsider that road now in the context of postmodern yearnings for authentic relationships.

This book presses beyond Christology to the deeper ground of Spirituality–the Trinitarian communion of the relational God. It thus builds on Allen's earlier book, *The Cruciform Church*, and presses readers to reflect on the meaning of fellowship with God. This is a welcome addition to our literature and the first to robustly explore the meaning of Trinitarian theology for Spirituality in Churches of Christ."

> —**JOHN MARK HICKS**, Professor of Theology, David Lipscomb University, Nashville, TN; author of *Yet Will I Trust Him: Understanding God in a Suffering World* (1999)

"Here is a very clear and relevant case study of the shaping impact of 'secular' philosophies on Christian theology. With particular reference to the Churches of Christ tradition, Leonard Allen and Danny Swick recall a crucial crossroads faced by this tradition in the 1850s, a crossroads critical both then and now. The unfortunate decision then was to favor a 'modernist' Lockean philosophy that, while employed to support renewed biblical faithfulness, led to an essentially Spiritless Christianity. Reverence for Scripture was burdened with a relationally impoverished philosophy of modernism. In varying degrees, much of establishment evangelicalism in the twenty-first century suffers from a similar impoverishment.

Robert Richardson was a prophet of the Spirit among the Churches of Christ in the nineteenth century—a story well told in these pages. Clark Pinnock, Stanley Grenz, and now Leonard Allen and Danny Swick assume this crucial prophetic role in the twenty-first century. May these voices be heard well. They are seeking to place Scripture back into the dynamic hands of the Spirit of God from whence it originally came and to newly highlight life transformation and discipleship as the enduring reasons for the very existence of the Bible."

> —**BARRY CALLEN**, Professor of Christian Studies, Anderson University; author of *Radical Christianity: The Believers Church Tradition in Christianity's History and Future* (Evangel, 1999), and editor of the *Wesleyan Theological Journal*

"One of the ironies of the Stone-Campbell movement is that many of its advocates have recently found themselves serving as the great defenders of certain tenets of modern philosophy. This irony is not lost on Allen and Swick, who suggest that this strange loyalty stems from a fateful decision a century and a half ago when pivotal figures in the movement took the churches down a path so committed to the 'dirt philosophy' of Locke and Bacon that it unwittingly eclipsed the movement's commitment to biblical doctrine, especially with regard to the role of the Holy Spirit. The authors retrace that path, showing that the movement could have taken–and might once again take–a different path, one both more biblical and more open to the work that the Spirit of God desires to do in our lives. A must-read for all those in the Stone-Campbell movement who have long desired to welcome the Spirit back into the churches.

—**PHILLIP KENNESON**, Professor of Theology, Milligan College, Johnson City, TN; co-author of *Selling Out the Church: The Dangers of Church Marketing* (Abingdon, 1997)

"We in the Churches of Christ are at a crossroad, as Allen and Swick so persuasively claim. If we are to survive as a religious movement, we will have to go back and revisit previous crossroads in our history, seeking direction and recovery of truths we once knew. One such critical moment was the struggle in 1857 between Robert Richardson and Tolbert Fanning in the pages of the *Millennial Harbinger* and the *Gospel Advocate*. At stake was whether God's life would flow into ours empowering us to live extraordinary lives. Or would we remain locked in a way of thinking that actually undermines the goals of a full restoration of Christianity? This book will startle some and bewilder a few, but it is undeniably truthful. It will richly reward a careful reading by church leaders and all others who are devoted to Jesus and his church in our time. If the gospel light that is part of our honorable heritage continues to shine in the future, it will be because books like this were read and heeded."

—**DALE PAULS**, preaching minister, Stamford Church of Christ, Stamford, Connecticut

Participating in God's Life

C. LEONARD ALLEN
DANNY GRAY SWICK

PARTICIPATING IN GOD'S LIFE

Two Crossroads for Churches of Christ

NEW LEAF BOOKS / ORANGE, CALIFORNIA

PARTICIPATING IN GOD'S LIFE
published by New Leaf Books

Copyright 2001 by C. Leonard Allen

ISBN 0-9700836-4-5
Printed in the United States of America

Cover illustration: Scala/Art Resource, NY
Illustration design: The ColorEdge, Costa Mesa, CA

For information:
New Leaf Books, 12542 S. Fairmont, Orange, CA 92869
1-877-634-6004 (toll free)

02 03 04 05 06 07   9 8 7 6 5 4 3 2 1

To
David & Rachel Dillman

and

Charles & Roma Swick

who live the Trinitarian faith

we meant to write

He has given us his very great and precious promises, so that through them you may participate in the divine nature and escape the corruption in the world.

2 Peter 1:4

It is a cardinal feature of this religious reformation, to direct the attention of men to words, even to the precious words of Holy Scripture. But it was never intended that these should be made a substitute for the things they reveal, or that mere grammar and logic should replace spiritual discernment, and be permitted to establish themselves as a barrier between the soul and spiritual enjoyment.

Robert Richardson (1857)

You know always in your heart that you need God more than everything; but do you not know too that God needs you—in the fullness of His eternity needs you? How would man be, how would you be, if God did not need him, did not need you? You need God, in order to be—and God needs you, for the very meaning of your life....The world is not Divine sport, it is Divine destiny. There is Divine meaning in the life of the world, of human persons, of you and me. Creation happens to us, burns itself into us, recasts us in burning—we tremble and we are faint, we submit. We take part in creation, meet the Creator, reach out to Him, helpers and companions.

Martin Buber
I and Thou (1958)

Table of Contents

Expanded Table of Contents

Part III. An Alternate Road

Conclusion

Preface

This book continues the theological project begun in my earlier books, particularly *The Cruciform Church* (1990). Readers familiar with this work will recognize certain themes developed there. This book might best be described as an historical/doctrinal study of Spirituality in the heritage of Churches of Christ. As such, it addresses those whose faith and doctrine were formed by this particular American Christian tradition. I also hope that, as a case study in the impact of modern philosphy on Christian theology, the book will prove instructive and encouraging to Christians from various other traditions as we all face the shakedown of a new cultural era.

Churches of Christ originated in the two "restoration" movements begun by Barton W. Stone and Alexander Campbell in the early nineteenth century. Both men were Scotch-Irish Presbyterians who capitalized upon the new American impulse to clear away the "rubbish of the past" and return to a simple, original Christianity. Their two movements united in 1832 and were variously called Disciples of Christ and Churches of Christ. By the late nineteenth century a major division was in place: the more conservative, rural and southern Churches of Christ, and the more progressive, urban and northern Disciples of Christ. Through the mid-twentieth century, Churches of

Christ experienced steady growth but since the 1960s have entered a period of ferment, change and, it now appears, decline.

This book was conceived following a period of extensive research into several little-known episodes in the 1850s, episodes that I came to see as deeply revealing for Churches of Christ, not only in their historical development but also in their present upheavals. During this time Danny Swick and I were in frequent dialogue. He did some perceptive and challenging research of his own into the episodes that form the historical basis of this book. Over the several years that followed we gradually blended our thinking and writing into this present form.

It may annoy the historically minded, especially those of the modern variety, that our historical interest gets mixed in thoroughly with theological prescription and spiritual passion. And it may annoy the theologically and spiritually minded, especially those of the postmodern variety, that our spiritual passion is weighted by so much historical detail. But we don't mind being annoying. And it just may be that a certain kind of annoyance is one of the more important things we can do for our readers.

When referring to Christian Spirituality in this book we have chosen to capitalize the word in order to emphasize the central role of the Spirit of God. The term "spirituality" is used so loosely and vaguely today, and often in neo-pagan or simply psychological terms, that we want to highlight the distinctive and essential focus of Christian Spirit-uality—a kind of life made possible by the Spirit of God. We want to distance the word from contemporary usage where "spiritual" typically refers to something vaguely religious, mystical or non-material—or is used loosely to mean something like "the inner life" of a person. By capitalizing the word "Spiritual" we want to underscore its Pauline sense (he uses it as an adjective 24 times): "that which belongs to, or pertains to, the Holy Spirit"; "an adjective referring primarily to the Spirit of God."

I am grateful for the partnership of Danny Swick in this work. He was a student in several of my classes and completed his MA in theology under my direction. I can say without overstatement that he was one of the very finest students I have had the privilege of teaching. I am also honored and blessed by his friendship.

We hope that this book provides fresh and challenging glimpses into fuller participation in and enjoyment of God's Life, both for those who share the heritage of Churches of Christ and for those rooted in other Christian traditions.

C. Leonard Allen
December 2000

Acknowledgements

We gratefully acknowledge the kind assistance of the following people in the preparation of this volume: Phillip Kenneson of Milligan College, Johnson City, Tennessee; Terry Koonce of Houston, Texas; J. McDonald Williams of Dallas, Texas; George Bragg of San Juan Capistrano, California; John Arlotti of Irvine, California; Darryl Tippens, Provost of Pepperdine University; Mike Cope of Abilene, Texas; Edward Fudge of Houston, Texas; Stan Hollon of Tustin, California; Dale Pauls of Stamford, Connecticut; Royce Hunter of Dallas, TX; Tom Lightvoet of Costa Mesa, California; Kris Miller of South Bend, Indiana; and Roma and Charles Swick of Lake Jackson, Texas. In addition we would like to thank the following for their careful reading of the manuscript: Randy Consford, Mark Dean, Pierce Dean, Dean Fitch, Hilary Harrell, Daniel Napier, and Jeff Scott.

Introduction

The collapse of modernity's brass dome,
and the spiritual hunger that has arisen in
the aftermath, presents a sharp challenge to
Western Christians who have long lived in its
shadow. We are being pressured to face our
accommodations to and compromises with the
modernist demands, and to begin recovering
doctrine and practice that quietly fell out of
place. The pressure is good for us.

1

The Spiritual Journey Today

Today Churches of Christ are approaching the two-century mark in their journey as a modern Christian tradition. It is a momentous time. Western culture is undergoing a dramatic cultural and worldview shift that rivals—and may well surpass—the upheavals of the fourth and fifth centuries when the Roman empire was Christianized and of the fifteenth and sixteenth centuries when the modern world was born.

Such times are dizzying and traumatic. The ground under our feet shifts and rolls. We may not be able to explain the geology of the quakes and fissures. But we feel them. We know something is happening. And we easily lose our balance and our bearings.

Here at the two-century mark in their journey as a distinct people, Churches of Christ stand at a crossroad. It is a Spiritual crossroad. Or more accurately, a crossroad where different theologies of the Spiritual Life meet and diverge.

Churches of Christ have visited this Spiritual crossroad—or one very much like it—at least once before in their long journey. That was almost a hundred and fifty years ago, though the memory of that place and the choice of roads has been almost entirely forgotten.

In this book we will visit and describe these two crossroads, beginning with the second one—the one facing us now.

"Desperately Seeking Spirituality"

One of the most surprising and most visible features of the present time is the new spiritual openness and hunger. Our culture is marked by a huge spiritual hunger, in itself a telling sign of a major cultural shift. This spiritual interest, to be sure, is a mixture of gullibility, serious searching, silliness, brokenness, hucksterism and desperation. Not so much a "culture of disbelief" (as Stephen Carter's book title puts it) as a culture of intense, eclectic and confused spiritual searching.

The modern world (call it modernity, for short) desiccated the human spirit, almost drained the soul dry. Now postmoderns are trying, in almost every imaginable way possible, to restore their shriveled souls. This search for the soul, however, is joined with a fairly widespread rejection of, or at least disinterest in, traditional, institutional Christianity as offering the kind of spirituality that can satisfy the hunger. Summarizing a recent body of statistical data, Leonard Sweet states that Americans "are exhibiting the highest interest in spiritual matters in 50 years, and Christianity is registering the least amount of interest and energy in 50 years."[1] The title of a 1994 *Psychology Today* article captured the mood: "Desperately Seeking Spirituality."

Nowhere is the character of today's spiritual landscape seen more starkly than on Amazon.com. I recently browsed their main web page on "Spirituality" and found four featured books. One was *Verses from the Center: A Buddhist Vision of the Sublime*. Calling the author "a purveyor of agnostic Buddhism," Amazon's blurb announced that he "faces the emptiness of existence and comes out brimming with authenticity." Another was *How to Know God: The Soul's Journey into the Mystery of Mysteries*, by Deepak Chopra, an endocrinologist with an Irish Catholic upbringing now purveying an eclectic blend of Hinduism and New Age mysticism.

Two other books rounded out the feature page. *God, Creation, and Tools for Life* (Amazon sales rank #151), written by a psychic and founder of a church based on heretical Christian Gnosticism who claims to convey spiritual wisdom through a spirit guide and through her "psychic grandmother." Finally, there was a book on Jewish mysticism entitled *God Was in This Place and I Did Not Know: Finding Self, Spirituality, and Ultimate Meaning,* by Lawrence Kushner.

Numerous indicators point to the dramatic new interest in things spiritual. Since 1995 almost 1000 books with the word "soul" in the title have been published. In the spring of 1998 seven of the top ten books on the New York Times nonfiction bestseller list were about spirituality. Sales of New Age books went from 5.6 million in 1992 to 9.7 million in 1995. The largest-drawing lecturer in recent years at Drew University in New Jersey was not Colin Powell or a presidential candidate but Deepak Chopra (tickets started at $40). Among its nine special interest book clubs, the Book of the Month Club's "One Spirit" has been the fastest growing in the company's history.[2] And perhaps most telling of all, the television soap operas, where for 30 years and more there was not a sign of any spiritual yearnings at all, have recently begun to portray their characters as actually having spiritual lives.

The young people of the first postmodern generations—the Generation Xers and the Net-Gens—are especially caught up in the spiritual quest. A recent study of the first college graduating class of the new millennium (the class of 2001) showed that 9 in 10 believe in God, 75% believe in life after death, 57% attend religious services, and 45% say that religion will be even more important to them in the future—figures considerably higher than the general population.[3]

Surveying the cultural signs of spiritual hunger, Leonard Sweet concludes: "A spiritual tsunami has hit postmodern culture. This wave will build without breaking for decades to come. The wave is this: People want to know God. They want less to know about God or know about religion than to know God. Postmoderns want something more than new products; they want new experiences, especially new experiences of the divine."[4]

Eugene Peterson, a pastoral theologian and keen observer of spiritual life in America, recently wrote: "There is a groundswell of recognition spreading throughout our culture that all life is at root spiritual, that everything we see is formed and sustained by what we cannot see. Those of us who grew up during the Great Spiritual Depression and who accustomed ourselves to an obscure life in the shadows of arrogant and bullying Technology can hardly believe our eyes and ears. People all around us—neighbors and strangers, rich and poor, communists and capitalists—want to know about God."[5]

A recent study by sociologist Robert Wuthnow illumines the nature of this new spirituality in American culture. Working from a large number of extensive interviews, Wuthnow describes a sea-change in American spiritual life. At the dawn of the twentieth century, he says, most Americans lived out their faith in a Jewish or Christian framework; they were cradle-to-grave members of their traditions. They attended services regularly and supported the institutional expressions of their faith. This pattern prevailed down through the religious revival of the 1950s. But in the latter decades of the twentieth century, according to Wuthnow, that prevailing pattern of spirituality has been undergoing deep change.

Seeking to conceptualize this shift at a level well beyond statistics on church attendance and membership, Wuthnow argues that a "spirituality of seeking" is supplanting a more traditional "spirituality of dwelling." The traditional spirituality emphasized habituation. God occupied a definite place in the world and created a space or home where people can dwell and feel secure. A spirituality of seeking, in contrast, emphasizes negotiation, where people explore new, often confusing and conflicting, horizons. Finding themselves in strange territory, they pick and choose among complex and competing versions of the sacred.

The one is "temple religion" located in the Promised Land, and characterizes the time of kings and priests; the other is "tabernacle religion" located in the Diaspora and looking to prophets and judges. The one has carefully maintained forms and boundaries; the other negotiable forms and porous boundaries. The one holds an orderly, systematic understanding of reality; the other a more partial and pragmatic view. The one looks favorably upon institutions, viewing them as the strong building blocks of society and the places that provide status and make productive work possible; the other looks less favorably upon institutions, placing networks and tasks over organizational protocol and position.[6]

This shift from dwelling to seeking, Wuthnow argues, marks our present culture. Both in the social realm and in the spiritual realm, images of traditional and settled dwellings have increasingly given way to images of homelessness. The migrant worker. The refugee. The vagrant. The lonely internet surfer. The alienated and displaced. And so also in affairs of faith and the spirit. Spiritual homelessness and vagrancy abound. And not only homelessness, but the very rethinking of what home is like and where it may be found.

The Collapse of the Brass Heaven

Why this vast upsurge in spiritual openness and seeking? Why now? The answer, in a word, is that the brass heaven has collapsed.

Over the last three centuries, the architects of the modern world gradually constructed a solid and impenetrable canopy that effectively shut out the invisible spiritual realm. Through the long rise of the secular and scientific worldview, a dome was erected over Western culture. It was solid and gleaming like brass, a grand and impressive structure. Its first effect was to create a great divide between the natural and the supernatural, and then eventually to seal off the heavens. It gradually dimmed and altered, then shut out light from the heavens. The world of the mechanized and the managed became the only world that mattered. Human autonomy replaced Divine Presence.

For more than two centuries Christians in the West lived in the deep shadow of the brass dome. They were constantly on the defensive against the steady encroachment of the secular and scientific worldview. Christian intellectuals and apologists, to varying degrees, sought to accommodate that worldview. They sought to reformulate faith—and tone down or banish its mysteries—so that it could pass modernity's all-important test: scientific rationality.

But now modernity's impenetrable brass dome has fallen under its own weight. The light of the heavens has come streaming in again. It's a new day. There is a new openness to the transcendent, invisible and spiritual realm. Non-Christians are squinting awkwardly in the light, looking hither and yon for its source. And professing Christians, long intimidated by the dome, are now able to embrace more readily the full wealth of historic Christian convictions, some of which—miracles, the Trinity, the reality of the "powers" and of Divine presence, for example—were readily sacrificed or compromised to accommodate modernity.

Take, for example, the realm of the powers and demons portrayed in Scripture. References to demons, angels and powers were widely regarded as myths by modern people—important perhaps for conveying some theological truth but not real. Even many conservative Christians, who are unwilling to call anything in the Bible "myth," have almost relegated this realm to that status. Their modern worldview simply did not allow for the kind of active (and interactive) spirit realm that is assumed in the Bible.

This situation presents those Christians who cling to a modern worldview with a dilemma: Jesus, Paul and the writers of the New Testament all thought that people could be inhabited by spirits—both evil and divine. "Whatever the modern explanation might be," New Testament scholar Marcus Borg wrote, "it must be stressed that Jesus and his contemporaries (along with people in most cultures) thought that people could be possessed or inhabited by a spirit or spirits from another plane. Their worldview took for granted the actual existence of such spirits."[7] Yet the modern Western worldview did not generally accept this assumption. Walter Wink, in his major study of the New Testament "powers," expressed this Western bias more bluntly than most: "It is as impossible for most of us to believe in the real existence of demonic or angelic powers as it is to believe in dragons, or elves, or a flat world."[8]

We face an unbridgeable gulf between the Bible's affirmation of the reality of the spirit realm and the modern, Western worldview.

The last 200 years or so is the only time in human history when the existence of such a spirit realm and our personal engagement with it has been widely doubted—and this skepticism spread only in Western societies. Most African, Asian and South American Christians—as well as those of the first postmodern generations—have no problem understanding or being open to Jesus' casting out of evil spirits or Paul's talk of "principalities and powers" or the biblical experience of Presence. It is modern European and American people who have tended to downplay, ignore or dismiss these forces.

But the modern worldview with its built-in secular biases and narrow view of what is real has been dislodged. Some say it has crumbled. As poet Christopher Fry put it:

> The human heart can go to the lengths of God.
> Dark and cold we may be, but this
> Is no winter now. The frozen misery
> Of centuries breaks, cracks, begins to move.
> The thunder is the thunder of the floes,
> The thaw, the flood, the upstart Spring.[9]

The reasons for this breaking apart are complex. To put it simply, the human spirit could not remain vigorous and strong while breathing the steadily thinning air of a secular worldview. As people climbed up the mountain of modernity the air got thinner and thinner, and they found themselves gasping for breath.

Furthermore, the modern age simply did not make good on its bold promises, especially the promise of steady progress toward social utopia. The "technological bluff"—the long-unquestioned conviction that technology will solve our problems—has been called. The prestige of scientific definitions of reality is diminishing; the invisible spiritual realm has again assumed the status of reality.

So the brass dome has collapsed. A good many Western people—especially intellectuals—do not yet know it. They are still huddled in the shadows of large chunks of the fallen dome. The bright light takes some getting used to if one has long lived in the shadows. But it is hard to miss or to ignore.

If the collapse of the brass heaven has brought a strong new spiritual interest to the culture as a whole, it has also brought, among Christians, a rediscovery of the rich and varied traditions of Christian Spirituality, ranging from the Desert Fathers, to Eastern Orthodoxy, to Pietism, to Wesleyan sanctification, to twentieth-century pentecostalism. Popular writers like Richard Foster, Dallas Willard, Henry Blackaby and Thomas Oden have mined this heritage in widely-read books. Respected evangelical leaders are calling Christians to a recovery of the Spiritual classics, with renewed focus on the inner and outer disciplines, meditation on and praying of Scripture, and liturgical practice ordered around the Christian calendar.[10] Books on the Spiritual life have proliferated, some of them theologically thin and faddish, but all of them together a sign of the Spiritual interest among Christian believers in this new era.

A notable part of this Spiritual revolution is the emergence of "new paradigm churches" that are no longer bound by the constraints of the brass dome. Sociologist Donald Miller, in his sympathetic study of these "new paradigm churches" that are revolutionizing American Protestantism, says that these churches are breaking sharply with modern assumptions about reality. His chief examples are the large networks of churches associated with Calvary Chapel, Vineyard Christian Fellowship and Hope Chapel. He calls these Christians "postmodern primitivists": postmodern in that they "refuse to absolutize the last 200 years of science-dominated thinking," and primitivists because they look to primitive or first-century Christianity for "a radical spirituality that undermines the cynicism and fragmentation of many postmodern theorists." "New paradigm Christians are quite comfortable," says Miller, "with an epistemology that breaks with critical thought and interjects God into everyday experience, denying the sacred-profane split" that became normative in the Enlightenment.[11]

The vast—and surprising—spiritual openness and searching of our time is part of the opening not only of a new millennium but of a new era in Western culture. And it will not soon diminish. "You may be sure," theologian Michael Novak wrote recently, "that the twenty-first century will be the most religious in five hundred years....We have come through a long and bloody century, and something new is stirring everywhere."[12]

The Journey of Churches of Christ

The collapse of modernity's brass dome and the spiritual hunger that has arisen in the aftermath, presents a sharp challenge to Western Christians who have long lived in its shadow. We are being pressured to face our accommodations to and compromises with the modernist demands, and to begin recovering doctrine and practice that quietly fell out of place and out of sight. The pressure is good and healthy for us.

This place is a Spiritual crossroad of sorts. New direction and new possibilities are intersecting old paths. Course corrections can be made, new direction chosen. We can allow God to rechart the course, reload the wagons, and perhaps get us back on the way we meant to go.

Churches of Christ, in their 200-year modern journey, now stand at this Spiritual crossroad. Because of their distinctive journey and the particular baggage they have born along the way, this present crossroad presents distinctive challenges. Our purpose in this book is to focus and understand these challenges—and to point to a way forward that can bring us more fully into the riches and enjoyment of God's Life.

Churches of Christ, no doubt, will continue to react against the trendy, fashionable—and often heretical—spiritualities of the time, the running after spiritual experiences, the syncretism, the charismatic hype and excesses portrayed in the media—and there will be considerable substance to their critique of these trends. Churches of Christ, after all, were born in sharp reaction against the experiential free-for-all of the early American revivals. But our own theological tradition, which has tended to be reactionary rather than constructive, ill-equips us for the recovery of a robust and balanced Spirituality after the fall of the brass heaven.

In recent years many members of Churches of Christ have begun tasting the new spiritual fare, no doubt out of curiosity, but certainly out of their own Spiritual hunger also. A good number have been drawn, for example, to the wave of small groups studying material like Henry Blackaby's *Experiencing God* (1992) that comes out of the Baptist "deeper life" Spiritual tradition,[13] to books like Richard Foster's *Prayer: The Heart's True Home* (1994) with roots in Quaker Spirituality, and to the Walk to Emmaus retreats which have quickened the Spiritual lives of many thousands. And we suspect that the appeal of the Promise Keepers' rallies owes as much to powerful—and to many men in Churches of Christ, quite new—experiences of God in worship as to the calls to strengthen and renew family commitments. No matter that these materials and these theologies clash sharply with some of the basic theological tenets of Churches of Christ; indeed, the embrace of these materials and events can be seen as a kind of grassroots critique of a tradition devoid both of language to talk about "experiencing God" and a theological framework able to account for and discipline such experience.

After the fall of the brass dome, it is not that Churches of Christ need to "get in step" with the postmodern culture and adopt its vocabulary and interests so they can be more relevant and attractive to the denizens of this strange new age; rather, it is that the challenges of this new era can reopen doors to Christian truth and experience that were closed or seldom used in modernity and lead to the reintroduction of Christian practices that have atrophied in its thin air. The jarring and shaking of these times can awaken Christians to a more faithful and robust practice of their faith and to a fuller confession of its historic truth.

For Churches of Christ this present crossroad is in a certain sense, as we noted earlier, a *deja vu* experience. For much earlier in our journey we faced a similar crossroad. That first crossroad was quickly passed and the memory of it largely lost, for there was not then the worldview shakeup and dizzying passages that today demand our attention and will hardly let us journey forward on business as usual.

We turn in the next chapter to tell the story of that first crossroad and to assess what it meant for the Spiritual journey of Churches of Christ.

Notes

1. Leonard Sweet, *SoulTsunami: Sink or Swim in New Millennium Culture* (Grand Rapids, MI: Zondervan, 1999), 410; *Trends Journal* (Spring 1997).

2. See Lynn Garrett, "Notes from the Marketplace: Booksellers Continue to See Steady Growth in the Sale of Religion and Spirituality Titles and Look Forward to More of the Same," *Publishers Weekly* (November 10, 1997), 32-37, and Michael F. Brown, *The Channeling Zone: American Spirituality in an Anxious Age* (Cambridge: Harvard University, 1997).

3. "Generation 2001: A Survey of the First College Graduating Class of the New Millennium," http://www.Northwesternmutual.com/2001.

4. Sweet, *SoulTsunami*, 420.

5. Eugene Peterson, *Subversive Spirituality* (Grand Rapids: Eerdmans, 1994, 1997), 33.

6. Robert Wuthnow, *After Heaven: Spirituality in America since the 1950s* (Berkeley: University of California, 1998), 1-18.

7. Marcus Borg, *Jesus, A New Vision* (New York: Harper & Row, 1987),

8. Walter Wink, *Naming the Powers: The Language of Power in the New Testament* (Philadephia: Fortress, 1984).

9. Christopher Fry, *A Sleep of Prisoners* (London: Oxford, 1951), 47.

10. See Richard J. Foster, *Streams of Living Water: Celebrating the Great Traditions of Christian Faith* (San Francisco: Harper San Francisco, 1998), and Robert Webber, *Ancient-Future Faith: Rethinking Evangelicalism for a Postmodern World* (Grand Rapids: Baker, 1999), 117-38.

11. Donald E. Miller, *Reinventing American Protestantism: Christianity in the New Millennium* (Berkeley, CA: University of California, 1997), 25, 125.

12. Michael Novak, "The Most Religious Century," *New York Times* (May 24, 1998).

13. On Blackaby and the "deeper life" tradition, see Gary Furr, "'The Road of

Ashes': Spirituality and the Prospects for Disillusioned Baptists," in *Ties That Bind: Life Together in the Baptist Vision,* ed. Gary A. Furr and Curtis W. Freeman (Macon, GA: Smyth and Helwys, 1994), 127-49.

Part I

At the Crossroads, 1857-60

In the late 1850s two roads came together, crossed one another, then quickly diverged in different directions. So quickly was the cross-road passed that the memory of it scarcely remains among Churches of Christ. This section revisits that crossroad, assesses what was at stake in the choice of roads and begins to explore the road not taken.

2

The Road Not Taken

The first Spiritual crossroad for Churches of Christ occurred in the late 1850s. It was the eve of the Civil War and strong sectional tensions had been driving a wedge between Northern and Southern churches for some time. For over a decade there had been growing tension over organizational and doctrinal issues. The Civil War period has thus been seen as a fork or crossroad from which open division between Churches of Christ and Disciples of Christ later emerged.

But we speak here of a different crossroad, one that has not been widely recognized. It was a theological and Spiritual, not a sociological or organizational, crossroad. Two roads came together, crossed one another, then quickly diverged in very different directions. So quickly was the crossroad passed that the memory of it scarcely remains among Churches of Christ. This chapter revisits that crossroad, maps the two roads and begins to explore the road not taken.

This theological crossroad emerged most clearly in the 1857 written exchange between Robert Richardson, associate editor of the *Millennial Harbinger* in Bethany, West Virginia, and Tolbert Fanning, founding editor of the *Gospel Advocate* in Nashville, Tennessee. The exchange was provoked when Fanning responded to a series of articles by Richardson entitled "The Misinterpretation of Scripture." In the series Richardson had argued that one does not properly interpret the Bible by a merely "formal" or rational reading of it. Rather, he insisted that the Spiritual truth contained in the Bible must be received, not merely with the understanding, but with the spirit or heart. Fanning went on the attack, calling the articles "purely metaphysical" and designed to "introduce novelties among the brethren."[1] This attack provided the occasion for Richardson to write a series of ten articles entitled "Faith versus Philosophy," to which Fanning replied in a series of six articles.[2]

The controversy that erupted around these articles was complex, damaging and deeply revealing. It was damaging to Richardson personally and to the movement collectively. Since this story is not well known, we will narrate it here.[3] But most basically we are after the two theological mindsets represented by these two men. Our larger concern is the way this episode reveals fundamental theological and Spiritual issues, and how we might reconsider those issues today as Churches of Christ stand at a new crossroad.

The controversy, in essence, was the clash of two incompatible theologies. At its heart was debate over a particular philosophy which had been deeply woven into the theological fabric of the movement since its early days. Richardson believed that this philosophy distorted the basic character of the Christian faith and seriously undermined Spirituality, thereby impeding a fuller restoration of New Testament Christianity. Fanning believed that this "philosophy" (which he denied was a philosophy at all) was necessary to preserve true Christian faith against the dangerous threats of mysticism.

Standing at the crossing of these roads in 1857-60, Churches of Christ, as we will see, overwhelmingly chose Fanning's road. Richardson's became a soon forgotten side road—the road not taken. We turn now to explore this crossroad and what was at stake in the choice of roads.

The Serpent in the Garden

When Richardson began his "Faith versus Philosophy" series in March 1857 he had been living in Bethany, West Virginia, and working closely with Alexander Campbell for 21 years. He was a medical doctor by training (and the Campbell's family physician), professor of chemistry at Bethany College, associate editor of the *Millennial Harbinger* (for which he had written regularly since its beginning in 1830), and a close friend of Campbell. A somewhat quiet and retiring man, he was deeply respected throughout the movement and widely viewed as one of its most eloquent and thoughtful writers. After Campbell's death he was asked by the family to chronicle Campbell's life and career, and the biography that resulted remains the standard to this day.

In 1857 Tolbert Fanning, age 47, had been a moving force in the Nashville church since 1840. He was a preacher, educator and editor. He had founded Franklin College in 1845 and the *Gospel Advocate* in 1855. Like Richardson, Fanning also deeply admired Campbell. Twenty years earlier (in 1835 and 1836) he had accompanied Campbell on two long preaching tours and afterwards had spent a season in his Bethany home. Standing six feet six inches tall and weighing 240 pounds, Fanning was as powerful and commanding a leader as he was a physical specimen.

Though the 1857 series seems to have been provoked by Fanning's attacks, the basic issues Richardson addressed were longstanding concerns. For him one of the most basic was Spirituality—the "real communion" with God made possible by the indwelling Spirit. Fifteen years earlier in 1842 and 1843 he had published a series of seven articles on "The Spirit of God" where he had voiced his concerns. He noted four current positions. (1) At one extreme were those who denied the Holy Spirit, and at the other (2) those who made everything depend upon the reception of the Spirit. In between these two extremes were two intermediate positions: (3) those who affirmed the presence of the Spirit in Christians but supposed the Spirit to be only "the effect of the word of God—the influence which the Scriptures produce upon the mind of the believer"; and (4) those who believe in "the reception of the Spirit in his own person, character and office."

Against Campbell and the tide of the movement's thinking, which was clearly running in the third category, Richardson affirmed the fourth position, that the "Holy Spirit of God is imparted to the believer, really and truly, taking up his abode in his person, as a distinct guest." He believed that Campbell and others, in rightly opposing the extremists of the second group, had overreacted and been driven into a practical denial of the Spirit's real presence and power. Certainly they talked of both the Spirit and the Word, Richardson said, but they put THE WORD in capital letters and (the Spirit) in parentheses, thus advocating in effect the false position that "the Spirit works only through the word of truth."[4]

At the very time in 1842 and 1843 when Richardson was publishing these articles, he and Campbell—close friends and longtime co-workers—were having vigorous discussions over these very issues. Campbell was preparing for his debate with N. L. Rice (which began in November 1843) where he had agreed to defend the proposition that "in conversion and sanctification the Spirit works only through the word of truth." Richardson had tried to persuade him not to defend such a proposition or at least not to limit God's working by attaching the word "only."[5]

Such a view, Richardson believed, chilled Spiritual vitality and replaced it with a doctrinal formalism, thus arresting the full restoration of pure Christian faith. Throughout the 1840s and 50s he continued to address these issues in his many writings. By 1857, with the movement's theology hardening and his concern of many years unabated, Richardson decided to take a bold step. He determined to address explicitly and openly what he believed to be the underlying root of the Spiritual concerns he had been addressing over the years.

There are "earnest and thoughtful individuals," he began, "who fear that the true temple of God has not yet been restored to these foundations; or that, if built, it has not, as yet, been filled with the Divine presence." Richardson made it very clear that he counted himself among this group. Something had gone awry in the movement, and the problem lay in one of three things: (1) there was some defect in the basic principles of the movement; (2) the principles have not been applied properly; or (3) "some system of human philosophy has insidiously intruded itself, and, like the serpent in Eden, seduced the unwary, by the charms of forbidden knowledge."

As to the first possibility, Richardson asserted that the basic principles are sound, indeed that they contain not the slightest flaw. These include Scripture as the only guide, rejection of tradition as binding, Scriptural authority for every practice, and freedom of conscience. As to the second possibility, Richardson asserted that in the application of these principles to the preaching of the gospel, to the practice of believers' baptism, and to the ordering of the church there has been no deficiency. Indeed, he claimed that theirs was the only body professing these principles "in their primitive purity and simplicity."

Yet here in the matter of applying the founding principles the problem begins to be revealed. Our purpose, he said, has been to "restore pure primitive apostolical Christianity in letter and spirit; in principle and practice." This is a great work. Who will presume to say it is fully accomplished? We have maintained that it is effected so far as the "letter" and the "principle" are concerned, but who will affirm that primitive Christianity is fully exhibited in "spirit" and in "practice"? Something was blocking the Spiritual life and practice of the movement, Richardson insisted. The movement was effectively making many "proselytes" but somewhere in it there remained a "serious defect, which paralyzes the most earnest efforts, and renders comparatively fruitless the most successful proselytism." Some were saying that the problem was lack of sufficient organization, that they needed more shepherds to tend the flock and a better system of church cooperation using districts and conventions. But, Richardson said, "it is not organization that can impart life. It is not the election of officers or the giving to them the titles of pastors or elders that can reanimate a dying church." The more basic problem is "spiritual sterility," the absence of Divine Life or energy.

Yes, something had gone awry in the movement, but the problem lay at a level much deeper than most supposed. The problem in fact lay primarily in the third possibility mentioned above: a human philosophy had infiltrated the camp, blocking the flow of Divine Life and leaving many content with "a mere formal profession" of Christianity. The basic problem was "the introduction of theories and speculations in direct violation of the very fundamental principles of this Reformation." Pure faith had been adulterated by human philosophy, not openly, not in formal propositions or creeds, but subtlely and insidiously in the very foundation of the edifice. As a result the basic principles of restoration operated with a lack of Spiritual power.

The proponents of restoration, Richardson pointed out, long had recognized the neutralizing effects of human philosophy upon Divine truth, and how difficult it is to disentangle the two. So why should they consider themselves exempt from this pitfall? The contamination of faith with philosophy is a very subtle business. No one sets out to do it. Everyone thinks that his or her "speculations" are simply revealed Bible truths. But the fact is, Richardson insisted, that leading proponents of the "present Reformation" have become unconscious victims of a philosophy that is "as great a hindrance to spiritual progress as is any system of speculation in vogue among the religious parties of the day."

Tolbert Fanning provided Richardson with a ready example of this very tendency. Fanning had just written a series of articles in the *Gospel Advocate* denouncing all philosophy as inherently destructive to Christian faith. In the process he had charged Richardson with "infidelity" for embracing speculative philosophy.[6] But in his very denunciation of all philosophy, Richardson shows, Fanning had employed the philosophical theories of John Locke, the preeminent philosopher of the British Enlightenment.

Locke held that the human mind at birth is a blank slate and that all knowledge comes through the five senses. He held further that, since God and Spiritual things cannot be experienced by the five senses, we are entirely dependent upon the Bible for any knowledge of or contact with God. In short, the Bible and the five bodily senses provide the only pathway into the human soul. This system, Richardson noted, has appropriately been called the "dirt philosophy" due to its complete dependence upon material things.[7] And it is precisely the philosophy Fanning has adopted as a platform for his interpretation of the Bible—though he has condemned all philosophy as evil and claimed to be free of any such influences.

Richardson concluded that Fanning, though unconscious of it, is "a philosopher of the School of Locke, or, what is usually termed a sensualistic dogmatist." Indeed, the case of Fanning shows that it is very possible for a person thoroughly to embrace a human philosophy without having the slightest awareness of its profound influence.

In this expose of Fanning as one caught up in the Lockean or Baconian philosophy, Richardson found himself in a very delicate situation. For it was Alexander Campbell, far more than Fanning, who was responsible for the Baconian cast of the movement's theology. Richardson could say that bluntly in private, but in public his critique had to be indirect, for he was in a double bind. He deeply admired Mr. Campbell, saw him as a great and good pioneer of restoration, agreed with the foundational principles upon which he had set the movement, and, on top of that, was his junior colleague, close friend, and office manager for the *Harbinger*. But he had long been convinced that Campbell's philosophical stance was deeply compromising the very plea he had so effectively pioneered.

By 1857 he felt compelled to critique this clandestine philosophy more openly. And since he could not or would not direct it to Campbell himself, chose Fanning as a stand in. Even so, Richardson's articles would bring him much grief and place great strain on his long friendship with Campbell.

Richardson took this risky step because he felt so strongly about the harmful Spiritual effects of the "dirt philosophy." He believed that it struck at the heart of the Christian faith, distorting its essential nature, sapping its power and diminishing the enjoyment it brings.

By its very nature this philosophy "constantly seeks to resolve everything into sensation, or into mere words." Its effect is "to unfit men's minds to receive anything that is not merely outward and formal," and it is thus "naturally and directly antagonistic to everything spiritual in religion." It gradually "dries up the fountains of spiritual sympathy, and creates in the heart a species of impiety towards the spiritual and invisible which doubts its presence and denies its power, and thus substitutes, in religion, an interested obedience to things external, for the confiding heart-trust of unselfish love—an experience which is merely sensible and exterior, for the self-consciousness of the soul and the earnest of the Spirit." If pursued to its end, Richardson concluded, such a philosophy divests "faith of all its spirituality, and confin[es] it to the earth, like a bird which has been deprived of its plummage and is no longer able to mount towards the skies." The practical effect, in short, is Spiritual debilitation and a fixation on outward form.

The Germ of Religion

Richardson was particularly concerned about the way this philosophy distorted the nature of faith. One's understanding of faith determines one's view of the kind of relationship we have with God. Indeed, faith is "the very germ of religion," so that "a mistake here, however slight or even imperceptible at first, must necessarily issue in an ever widening divergence from the truth."

To clarify Richardson's concerns about the nature of faith, let's consider a bit of background. Near the heart of Campbell's movement (as a theological movement) was a particular understanding of the nature of faith and conversion. For many years Campbell had argued that conversion results from an unbreakable chain of cause and effect. It begins with "gospel facts," then testimony to those facts, then belief of this testimony (faith), then obedience, and then finally the gradual growth of the appropriate feelings or "affections." He insisted that where factual testimony begins, faith begins, and where testimony ends, faith ends. He said it scores of times: "No testimony, no faith; strong testimony, strong faith; weak testimony, weak faith; little testimony, little faith." Campbell could occasionally link faith to trust or confidence in a person, but the momentum of his thinking was strongly toward faith as acceptance of factual testimony. "Faith is neither testimony nor reason," he wrote in a typical remark, "but reason receiving testimony."[8]

Campbell had developed this view of faith and conversion in opposition to what he considered extreme and damaging views of "spiritual operations." Word and Spirit had been driven apart among many overheated believers, he believed, so he sought to stress the foundational role of the Word with its hard and secure "facts." The Lockean or Baconian philosophy proved a ready and effective weapon in this struggle.

Campbell's view of faith thus closely resembled Locke's definition: "Faith is the assent to any proposition not made out by the deductions of men, but upon the credit of the proposer as coming from God, in some extraordinary way of communication." When Fanning quoted this definition with hearty approval, Richardson was quick to point out that such a definition makes faith little more than an intellectual assent to the truthfulness of facts rather than trust in a person.[9] And this was the very problem that Richardson believed was paralyzing the movement's Spiritual progress.

Richardson did not wish to disparage in any way the facts upon which faith rests. Belief of testimony or of gospel "facts" is certainly necessary as a foundation for faith. And in the laying of this foundation the Lockean or Baconian focus upon "fact" could serve perhaps an important though limited function. But, Richardson argued, the setting of a foundation does not necessarily mean the erection of a proper building upon it. Factual testimony provides only the foundation of faith's house, and it is absolutely vital, to be sure. But faith itself is nothing more or less than "a trusting in Jesus, a personal reliance." Indeed, when Jesus commended people for their faith it was "because with a very moderate amount of evidence, there was exhibited a ready and confiding trust." Certainly growth in faith requires an increase in knowledge but it depends primarily upon the deepening of the heart's "affections" where one "enter[s] into fellowship with Christ, into the nearest and most intimate spiritual relations." Thus the normative act of faith is not accepting the gospel facts but rather entering into a trusting relationship with Christ.

But the "dirt philosophy" quickly distorts the nature of faith and arrests its proper growth. It exaggerates the power of facts, endows the words of the Bible with "unwonted efficacy," and improperly ties faith to material things. The strict Baconian cannot get beyond "facts" and arguments to an intimate and personal communion with God. He cannot get beyond the "letter" to the Spirit, or we might say that for him the "letter" is the only means of contact with the Spirit. Indeed, the reflex of this philosophy is "to resolve, so far as possible, everything into words, propositions, arguments, and to reduce all spiritual phenomena to the forms of the ordinary understanding."

The words, facts and information of Scripture are important. But they are means, not ends. Thus

> it is a cardinal feature of this religious reformation, to direct the attention of men to words, even to the precious words of Holy Scripture. But it was never intended that these should be made a substitute for the things they reveal, or that mere grammar and logic should replace spiritual discernment, and be permitted to establish themselves as a barrier between the soul and spiritual enjoyment. Yet this is precisely what is done under the influence of the sensualistic philosophy....So completely does our sensualistic philosopher occupy himself with words, that he can neither understand nor relish "the things of the Spirit." To him they are unacceptable "novelties."

Richardson did not disparage the material, the phenomenal and the factual, but he insisted that faith, properly speaking, involves much more. Faith, he insisted, does not terminate on the facts recorded, but these are record-ed that our faith might reach forward to something else—to something which is not recorded; to something which could not be recorded; to something which passes wholly beyond this wretched objective philosophy under view, even to the power, the love, the personal and official character of our blessed Redeemer himself, realized subjectively in the inner consciousness and affections of the soul.

To stop short of this and content oneself with the question, "Are the facts true?" is to stay "wholly destitute of the Christian faith." If faith is basically a belief of historical facts, then it quickly stagnates: it might increase in its extent (by believing more facts) but it cannot increase in degree, for "the facts can never be received as more than true." So once one sincerely believes the facts, faith, in this sense, reaches its fullness.

But such a view of faith is not Christian faith. Faith, properly understood, is a trusting in Christ, and such faith constantly grows as one experiences more and more of his love, wisdom and power. Growth in faith thus depends, not upon "mere declarations of ancient witnesses, but upon an actual and present Christian life, which itself springing from faith, produces faith, as the grain of corn produces the stalk which in turn produces the full corn in the ear."

With this view of faith Richardson was identifying with the clas-sical Christian understanding. Faith is prior. The role of reason or philosophy is to aid the understanding and perfecting of faith. From the "Divine stand-point," Richardson said, philosophy or the "reasons for things" precedes faith. But from the "merely human stand-point" we must reverse the order and say that "it is faith alone that can introduce us to this loftiest reason and philosophy, the possession of which is at once the fruit and the confirmation of our faith." Indeed, he asserts that "it is impossible that [one] should attain to faith through any philosophy, even the true one, much less by any system of mere human philosophy."

This classic view of faith was connected closely to a doctrine of the Spirit's illumination and personal indwelling. Strict Lockean or Baconian faith, in contrast, logically moved toward a "Word only" doctrine of the Spirit's presence. If divine agency is limited to the channel of the five senses and faith is fundamentally reason accepting testimony, then the Spirit will be understood as working only through revealed words. If on the other hand, faith in essence is a trusting relationship, then the Spirit can be understood as God's personal Presence.

At issue between Richardson and Fanning was the question, Does the Spirit comfort, guide and sustain Christians through means other than biblical words? Fanning answered with an emphatic no, and in the course of their exchanges finally revealed openly his strict Lockean or Baconian commitments:

> We profess no religious belief beyond what is written or "verbal." Words limit our confidence in religious truth. We also freely admit that we acknowledge none but a "formal" religion, and we can with good conscience call men infidels and profane scoffers at spiritual truth who profess anything beyond "verbal truth taught in words" or beyond the "formal religion of the Bible."

Richardson answered the question with an emphatic yes. For him the indwelling Spirit was the very source and power of the trustful relationship with God that one entered by faith. The Spirit was the real presence of God returned to indwell His temple, and that temple was the human heart and the church.

Fanning (following Campbell before him) argued that the Spirit's work is analogous to the change one's words or arguments make on the mind or spirit of another person. This was a serious error, Richardson judged, for with such a view one is actually saying that "there is no Spirit of God literally and really imparted, but merely a change effected in the human spirit." To the contrary, the Spirit is a real and abiding Presence to guide, comfort and renew. Further, though many admit the indwelling of the Spirit as a fact of Christian life, they do not know what it means in practice—it is "granted by words to the ear, but denied by Philosophy to the heart." And a gospel that comes in "word only" is not the gospel preached by Paul and the apostles.

Near the end of his series, after showing at length the "unhappy effects" of the Lockean philosophy, Richardson turned briefly to the opposite error: mysticism. The mystic accepts the Bible as Divine revelation but quickly grows impatient with its flat-footed and "ordinary" truths. He wants the extraordinary. He wants personal revelations and profound mysteries. He is put off by traditional channels of authority and tends to disregard outward forms.

Both the mystic and the Lockean distort Christian faith in equal measure, though from opposite directions. The Lockean believes too little, the mystic believes too much. The one collapses Spirit into Word, the other collapses Word into Spirit. The one "virtually rejects, by explaining it away, every passage of scripture that tends to spirituality," the other "regards the Christian ordinances and the written word itself as mere temporary expedients—scaffoldings for spiritual truth." The one is preoccupied with the outward and formal and is "naturally disposed to controversy," the other focuses on the inner life and deep things of God and "prefers quiet contemplation to debate." The one has the form of religion but lacks its power, the other seeks the power but is indifferent to the forms.

Richardson closed his "Faith versus Philosophy" series by affirming what he believed to be the original ideals of the movement. The "current Reformation" was built upon the rejection of human opinions, creeds and philosophies. We constantly attack and expose the "mystical philosophy" so entrenched among the various denominations, he said, yet ironically the Lockean philosophy has quietly, almost imperceptibly, and without protest entrenched itself in our theology. This philosophy, to be sure, is the opposite of the mystical one but is no less damaging to Spiritual growth and progress. For it numbs the spiritual sensibilities. It leaves people content with mere doctrines and forms of the faith. To uphold the foundational principles of the restoration movement, the philosophy that has blindsided them and compromised those principles must be exposed. "It will not do," he said, "to stop with baptism for remission of sins and leave the convert deprived by false philosophy of all true faith in the actual indwelling of the Holy Spirit, the impartation of which is the great end of gospel ministration, and which is the true source of spiritual life and power."

Fanning the Flames

Beginning with Richardson's fourth article, Fanning wrote a series of six sharp replies. To the charge that he was deeply tainted by the Lockean philosophy, Fanning's response was contradictory and at times incoherent. Though in an earlier writing he had praised Locke as the "real author of the Baconian philosophy, and all correct thinking in England since his day," he now asserted that Locke's system was only a "manner of thinking" and that Locke "was, strictly speaking, no philosopher" at all. Fanning strongly and angrily denied being a disciple of Locke, but toward the end of his reply states more forthrightly his Lockean commitments. He embraced Locke's definition of faith and, though he denied holding a "Word only" view of the Spirit's indwelling, he could make no coherent argument against it.

To Fanning's mind, Richardson's position was "unblushingly infidel," for he had abandoned the solid ground of revealed truth and embraced "modern spiritualism." This harsh charge by Fanning must be understood in light of an episode that had recently devastated the Nashville church and deeply wounded Fanning himself.

An eloquent young preacher named Jesse Ferguson had begun work with the Nashville church in 1846 and, under the encouragement and guidance of Fanning, led the church into rapid growth. But in 1852 Ferguson published an article arguing that people who rejected the gospel in this life would have an opportunity to receive it in the next. An intense controversy erupted. Campbell and others began a relentless attack, calling upon the brotherhood to reject such "leprous" teaching. Under this prolonged attack, Ferguson over the next two years moved further into objectionable views. By 1854 he had published a book embracing "spirit communion" or the ability to communicate with departed human spirits. A struggle over control of the Nashville church ensued, and by the time Ferguson finally resigned in 1856, the congregation had been laid waste. Fanning was devastated.

In 1857, therefore, Fanning was ready to turn his guns on anything that even hinted of Spiritualism. The "spiritualist," Fanning declared, is one who claims direct access to a higher spiritual realm. And as a result of this dangerous claim, the "spiritualist" soon shipwrecks his and others' faith. He ends up discounting Christ as the savior, renouncing the church as a saving institution, and rejecting the efficacy of Christ's ordinances.

Standing steadfastly against such "spiritualism," Fanning, as we have already seen, revealed clearly his fundamental Lockean premises. Richardson's response was that Fanning appeared to be "too deeply imbued with sensualistic philosophy to receive or comprehend the spiritual things of Christianity"; as a result, he was "unable to distinguish between modern spiritualism and ANCIENT SPIRIT-UALITY."

The Road Not Taken

Midway through the series tension began to mount between Campbell and Richardson as controversy over this issue spilled out in the movement. Campbell disapproved of Richardson's articles, and in September issued a rebuke: "we do not approve of philosophical disquisitions of any sort being presented to our readers in our monthly bills of fare. And as little do we approve of placing faith and philosophy in any real or formal antagonism."[10]

The tension deepened when a Baptist editor picked up on the controversy and wrote an article asking, "On Which Side Is Alexander Campbell?" In response Campbell attempted again to explain his view of faith. And he accused Richardson of being out of line in two things: his "choice of a subject" and "his manner of treating it."[11] Campbell basically assumed the awkward position of siding with Fanning, and this stance opened up a flood of attack upon Richardson. Richardson noted in a letter that Campbell "quietly suffered this to go on for months with only one or two slight and very imperfect corrections." He later commented that the "Faith versus Philosophy" series had brought him "the most bitter and unrelenting hostility in the form of misquotation, misrepresentation, and personal and professional distraction."[12]

Deeply distressed by these developments, Richardson in late 1857 resigned his editorial position with Campbell's journal and in February 1858 accepted a faculty position at the new Kentucky University. Campbell apparently was shocked. He urged Richardson to reconsider, and also printed an apology for supporting Fanning's charge that Richardson advocated a "Spirit-alone" theory. Affirming that Richardson's views were in keeping with those he had always promoted, Campbell rebuked Fanning, calling his effort to paint Richardson and others as heretics and infidels an "outrage" and the "grossest injustice." Fanning has become "super-excited," he said, and lost the ability to judge properly in these matters.[13] By January 1859 Richardson had accepted Campbell's offer to resume his editorial duties.

The breach with Campbell was repaired, and Richardson continued to be held in high regard by many leaders in the more northern part of the Restoration Movement. When Campbell died in March of 1866, Dr. Richardson was the one chosen to deliver the funeral sermon. He was also the one Campbell's family asked to write his biography. After three intense years of research and writing, Dr. Richardson completed the massive, two-volume *Memoirs of Alexander Campbell* in 1869. A few years before his death in 1876, Richardson published his book on the Holy Spirit entitled *A Scriptural View of the Office of the Holy Spirit* (1872), a work that may be the most sound and solid work on this doctrine the movement has produced.

Dr. Richardson remained in high esteem among many of the northern Disciples, and his view of faith and the Spirit continued to have influence there. But there too the Baconian underpinnings as set by Campbell remained more firmly in place than Richardson would have thought good.

The Road Taken

Tolbert Fanning was the undisputed leader of thought among southern churches up to the Civil War. His stand on these issues would set a dominant theological pattern. Not all of those who followed him down this path after 1857-58 were as starkly rationalistic in their views of faith and the Spirit, but the general emphases and ethos represented by Fanning would characterize the southern churches for over a century.[14]

Two examples from the twentieth century serve to show how enduring was this theological legacy. First is an influential book by Z. T. Sweeney entitled *The Spirit and the Word*, published in 1919. Sweeney argued that all of the work of the Comforter or Paraclete (as stated by Jesus in John 14-16) applied only to the twelve apostles, not to Christians in general. The Spirit as Comforter, he said, was a "private and peculiar" gift to the twelve for their one-time work of establishing the foundations of the church and producing inspired writings. Once this work of the Spirit was completed in the original apostles, "no man has been guided, shown and directed personally by him since." "God does no unnecessary work, and the work of the Paraclete is not necessary now. His work remains [only] in the teachings and lives of the apostles."

Sweeney echoed Campbell's (Lockean) theory that there are only two possible means by which one spirit (or Spirit) can influence another spirit: one is physically or immediately through the five senses, the other is rationally or morally through words and arguments. After the apostles and the inspiring of the New Testament, God's Spirit no longer works immediately but only mediately through words.

This assumption led Sweeney to a remarkable conclusion: many of the New Testament admonitions regarding the Spirit simply do not apply to Christians living after the first century. Some examples:

"You were sealed with the Holy Spirit of promise, which is an earnest of our inheritance" (Eph. 1:13, 14).

"Be filled with the Spirit" (Eph. 5:18).

"He saved us through the washing of regeneration and the renewing of the Holy Spirit" (Titus 3:5).

"He has given us of his Spirit" (1 John 4:13).

All of these verses, together with a long list of others, Sweeney insisted, must be interpreted as applying to first-century believers in whom God was "manifesting his presence by supernatural demonstrations"; but now that God works only through the words of Scripture these verses "lack meaning."[15]

Sweeney's book became a standard among Churches of Christ. It was reprinted by a major publisher serving Churches of Christ and went through many editions well past mid-century.

The second example is an episode that occurred in 1966 and 1967. Several speakers at the annual Abilene Christian University Bible Lectures in 1966 began to call for a renewed emphasis on the dynamic, though non-miraculous, influence of the Spirit in the Christian life. One said that "our lack of spiritual emphasis has dried up for many the spring of living water provided by the Holy Spirit, and people are thirsty." "One of the greatest weaknesses in our fellowship," said another, "has been our lack of understanding of the Holy Spirit."[16]

This raising of the "Spirit question" quickly touched a nerve, provoking an outburst of reaction that continued throughout 1966 and 1967. Reuel Lemmons, editor of the *Firm Foundation,* wrote several editorials warning about the dangers of raising such issues and reaffirming the traditional "Word only" view. Others wrote in a similar vein.

J. D. Thomas, of the ACU Bible faculty, responded, noting the unacceptable worldview implied in such a doctrine of the Spirit:

We must discount the idea of "biblical Deism," which assumes that God started the Christian system and left the

> Bible down here to do what it could, but meanwhile, He,
> Christ, and the Spirit have all retired to heaven and have
> nothing to do with the world until the end, when they will
> come back and check up to see how it all worked out.[17]

Thomas proceeded to lay out in a long series of articles a very
modest, cautious treatment of the Spirit in the life of the Christian.
He affirmed the Spirit's personal, actual indwelling, rejecting the
"Word only" view. He firmly rejected any new revelatory or miraculous activity of the Spirit. And he affirmed that we know of the
Spirit's personal indwelling, not from any physical effects the Spirit
may produce, but only because the Bible teaches it. Indeed, this
position retained the Lockean or Baconian assumption that all our
knowledge is gained empirically through the five senses.

Yet even so cautious an exposition of the doctrine of the Spirit
as this provoked strong and alarmed response from prominent
leaders. Reuel Lemmons feared that such a view means that the
Spirit can work in "an independent instantaneous, miraculous way
unconnected with the word of God." Another writer, also fearing
that direct influence or indwelling would open Pandora's "pente-
costal box," insisted that the Spirit works only in "an indirect, medi-
ate, natural, understandable manner." He set forth the remarkable
conclusion that both the Spirit and Satan no longer affect us super-
naturally but are both "restricted to the use of 'natural means.'"

Foy Wallace, Jr., long a garrulous defender of the "Word alone"
theory, entered the fray and starkly restated Campbell's (and
Fanning's and Sweeney's) position: "Apart from the inspiration of
the apostles and prophets, it is impossible for spirit to communicate
with spirit except through words. God and Christ never personally
occupied anyone; and for the same reason the Holy Spirit does not
personally occupy anyone."[18]

This 1960's debate was in several ways a rehash of 1857's
"Faith versus Philosophy" exchange. Behind this doctrine lay the
Enlightenment worldview shaped by the Lockean epistemology,
as mediated by Campbell, Fanning, Sweeney and others. Indeed,

the spirit of Locke haunts—or should we say "indwells"—the whole episode from beginning to end. What is missing in Sweeney's book of 1919 and in the 1960's reprise is any recognition or discussion of this fact. So deeply entrenched had this philosophy become that the sources of it had long been forgotten or lost; indeed, it had long functioned behind the scenes, at an unconscious, ideological level.

The fact that in 1966 an extremely cautious and unremarkable treatment of the Spirit's indwelling could call forth such painstaking and vigorous refutation provides a telling sign of the road taken by Churches of Christ. Certainly there had been a modest lineage of leaders who had affirmed a personal, immediate indwelling of the Spirit—people like Charles Roberson, G. C. Brewer, K.C. Moser and J. D. Thomas. But even there, as J. D. Thomas' 1966 exposition shows, the Lockean constraints had remained to some extent.

The matter that concerns us here, however, is much larger than the question of the mode of the Spirit's indwelling. That particular issue surfaced time and again, and provides perhaps the clearest and most direct sign of the hidden Lockean heritage. But this issue is only one piece of a whole theological mindset. Closely related, as Richardson pointed out in 1857, are issues of the nature of faith, the nature and source of the Spiritual life, and the character and purpose of prayer.

Behind these doctrinal issues (as Richardson only implied) lies the central Christian doctrine of the Trinity. The doctrine of the Trinity speaks of the character of God and of the way God enters into relationship with His creatures. It proclaims, not the passionless deity of Aristotle or the remote god of Enlightenment theism, but a God who is dynamic, demanding, personal and present. The chief problem with the hidden Lockean heritage among Churches of Christ lies precisely here: in its distorted or neglected or hobbled doctrine of the Trinity.

The affairs of 1857-58, we believe, stand as a kind of theological crossroads for Churches of Christ. We also believe that

Churches of Christ today stand again at a similar crossroads, a place where course corrections can be chosen, where there is openness to a new, more Spiritually vibrant path. By revisiting the road not taken in 1857, Churches of Christ, we believe, can see that path more clearly.

Notes

1. Tolbert Fanning, "Metaphysical Discussions—No. 2," *Gospel Advocate* 2 (1856), 328.

2. Robert Richardson, "Faith versus Philosophy—No. 1-10," *Millennial Harbinger* 4th ser. 7-8 (1857-58); Tolbert Fanning, "First-Sixth Reply to Professor Robert Richardson," *Gospel Advocate* 3 (1857).

3. For a fuller and more complete account of these events, including important episodes not touched on here, see Leonard Allen, *Things Unseen: How the Theology of Churches of Christ Brought Success in the Modern Age (and Why after Modernity It Probably Won't)* (forthcoming), chapter 4.

4. Robert Richardson, "The Spirit of God," *Millennial Harbinger* (1842-43).

5. Benjamin L. Smith, *Alexander Campbell* (St. Louis: Bethany Press, 1930), 328.

6. Fanning, "Metaphysical Discussions—No. 1-4," *Gospel Advocate* 2-3 (1856-57), 314-15, 326-29, 1-5, 31-38.

7. Richardson, "President Fanning's Reply," *Millennial Harbinger* 4th ser. 7 (1857), 433-34.

8. Campbell, "Opinionisms—No. 1," *Millennial Harbinger* 5th ser. 2 (1859), 434; Campbell, "Kingdom of Satan—No. 2," ibid. new ser. 2 (February 1838), 70.

9. John Locke, *An Essay Concerning Human Understanding*, ed. A. D. Woozley (New York: New American Library, 1964), 424; Fanning, "Fourth Reply to Professor Robert Richardson," *Gospel Advocate* 3 (1857), 281.

10. Campbell, "Christianity the True Philosophy—No. 1," *Millennial Harbinger* 4th ser. 7 (1857), 481.

11. Campbell, "The Religious Herald and Prof. Richardson," ibid., 577.

12. Goodnight and Stevenson, *Home to Bethphage: A Biography of Robert Richardson* (St. Louis, MO: Bethany, 1949), 176; Richardson, "Doctrine of the Spirit," *Millennial Harbinger* 5th ser. 1 (April 1858), 200.

13. Campbell, "A Correction," *Millennial Harbinger* 5th ser. 1 (1858), 289; Campbell, "President Fanning," ibid., 353. In his apology Campbell said: "I know

not how this misstatement could have occurred, unless that my writing the article away from home I had not an opportunity of examining Bro. Richardson's essay, and had probably before my mind some of those misquotations and misrepresentations of which he has complained." Campbell at this time also recognized the fact that this controversy was rooted in a struggle for power in the movement. The "truthful heading of the whole controversy, in spirit and form," Campbell wrote, would be "the 'Gospel Advocate' versus the 'Millennial Harbinger' and Franklin College versus Bethany College."

14. Earl West, in *The Search for the Ancient Order: A History of the Restoration Movement, 1809-1906* (Nashville: Gospel Advocate, 1949), 1:125ff., uncritically accepts Fanning's account of the exchange and clearly embraces Fanning's theological position. So also James Wilburn, *The Hazard of the Die: Tolbert Fanning and the Restoration Movement* (Austin, TX: Sweet, 1969). These works reflect the virtually complete triumph of Fanning's theological stance in the twentieth-century Churches of Christ.

15. Z. T. Sweeney, *The Spirit and the Word: A Treatise on the Holy Spirit in Light of a Rational Interpretation of the Word of Truth* (1919; reprint ed., Nashville, TN: Gospel Advocate, 1950), 67-79, 95-97, 99.

16. *Abilene Christian College Bible Lectures, 1966* (Abilene, TX: ACC Bookstore, 1966), 175-76, 185.

17. J. D. Thomas, *The Spirit and Spirituality* (Abilene, TX: Biblical Research Press, 1966), 19.

18. Reuel Lemmons, *Firm Foundation* 83, 722; ibid., 757; Foy Wallace, Jr., *The Mission and Medium of the Holy Spirit* (Nashville, TN: Wallace Publications, 1967), 7.

3

The Heart and the Matter

In the last chapter we introduced the characters, traced the plot, noted the factors propelling our two protagonists toward each other and indicated briefly why this very old debate is vitally relevant to our own day. Now we turn to probe deeper into the thought-worlds of the two primary characters and to explore further the crucial issues.

After outlining the conflict between Richardson and Fanning in the previous chapter, we also learned of the outcome: Richardson becomes disinherited from the southern part of the movement and Fanning becomes the new arbiter of orthodoxy in the south. But the story probably left more questions than answers. What was so controversial about Richardson's stand? Why was Richardson abandoned by friends and brethren, including Campbell himself, for what appeared to be rather modest claims about the work of the Spirit? Why was Fanning's inferior argument so appealing? And perhaps the most important question, what accounts for the fear that surfaces among the leaders of the Restoration movement in relation to this episode and its focal issue?

Let us take the last question first. But instead of addressing their fears let us first address our own. What follows in this chapter and succeeding ones may be labeled frightening by some. These chapters challenge the way many of us have grown accustomed to thinking. More to the point, Richardson's call to a faithful embrace of a Living God casts shadows on many of our accepted, comfortable and often dogmatic ideas. Richardson's claim, a claim we believe to be both true and relevant, is that nothing is more important than a living, dynamic relationship with God through the Holy Spirit.

This sounds safe enough, but it is not. If God's nearness to us is primary, then nothing should be allowed to stand in the way of that nearness. No doctrine of the Church, of the Spirit, of faith or even the Bible should inhibit or block the Presence of God in our lives. This, according to Richardson and as we shall later argue, is the teaching of the New Testament. Doctrine is certainly important but its importance must be reconsidered, redefined and reprioritized if we begin with God's empowering Presence.

The difficulty of the task will be overshadowed by the riches of a robust, balanced and biblical understanding of the Holy Spirit. Richardson traces a path within the Stone-Campbell tradition for such an understanding. His vision of restoration is one that never came to fruition because it was not able to be heard by many of his contemporaries. Today many are ready to consider an alternative vision. We may even find that it is precisely the vision we have been longing to see.

The Matter versus the Heart

Before exploring the key points of contention, we must look at the underlying point of contention. In any debate there are usually several subjects over which the two participants find themselves at odds, but there is also a more fundamental divergence in their thinking that gives rise to these different points. Beneath the disagreements about the role of Scripture in the Christian life, about experiential and intellectual faith, and about God's mode of involvement in our lives lies a more fundamental disagreement. In the case of Fanning and Richardson that point of contention lies with the place of Baconianism or John Locke's philosophy in the

Restoration Movement. Richardson claims that the insurgence of this philosophy in his day is largely reponsible for the distortion of key biblical doctrines and the waning of Spirituality in the tradition. He is more concerned, as we shall see, about the growing influence of the philosophy and the way it may inhibit Divine immediacy for future generations. This makes this old debate vitally interesting and relevant to the Restoration Movement today.

1) The Birth of the "Dirt Philosophy"
Enough has been written about the influence of this philosophy on the movement that we need not go into much detail here.[1] The most basic and central tenet of Locke's philosophy was that the mind is a "blank slate" that can only receive outside data. More simply, humans do not actually think up anything, they simply receive, organize and synthesize data from the outside world. For John Locke there is no such thing as an original idea.

This key point leads to a further, more significant conclusion for Locke and especially his Baconian followers. Since the human mind is completely passive and does not originate ideas in and of itself, it must collect its data from the visible or phenomenal world. The five senses are the exclusive vehicles for collecting this data. Thus one learns by collecting data from the visible world through the five senses. To answer the age-old question of what is real and what is illusory, Locke and his successors claimed that what can be touched, seen, heard, smelled and tasted defines what is real. Any thought we have can be traced back through a chain of ideas to some material we have sensed. Any thought which cannot be so traced, which is not grounded in the material world, is unreliable.

This philosophy, often called sensualistic (what one senses) materialism (information comes from matter) or more pejoratively the "dirt philosophy," seems rather harmless until one considers what it denies. The negative aspects of the philosophy are what most concerned Richardson and others who have attacked it. By dwelling on the phenomenal side of existence (what can be gained through the senses) it neglects the noumenal or imperceptible side.

It emphasizes the visible as the source of all knowledge, and reduces the invisible to the source of illusion and error. The philosophy becomes especially dangerous when it claims that all there is to reality is the stuff we can hear, see, touch, smell and taste. The danger will become clearer after we learn how Campbell used the philosophy.

2) The Application of the "Dirt Philosophy"

Campbell hammered out his theology on the anvil of American revivalism. He witnessed the highs and lows of the spirit of revivalism as it swept through America in its many phases, and it is against this background, or more precisely, in reaction to this background, that he fashioned his own brand of Christian Lockeanism.

It was the neurosis created by the revivals that so disturbed Campbell. At the heart of the revival movements was the conversion experience. It was widely believed and preached that God would act directly upon an individual if he or she had faith that God could do this. This action frequently took the form of a dramatic, emotional experience such as prolonged weeping or even convulsing. Believers and nonbelievers alike went to these revivals hoping for and indeed expecting an ecstatic encounter with the Living God. Often, however, individuals left the revivals more disheartened than when they arrived because the expected encounter never took place. For the disappointed it was easy to conclude that their faith was in some way defective; others anxiously awaited some action or experience that would relieve their doubts.

Campbell found the solution for these disenchanted believers in the application of Locke's sensualistic philosophy to Christianity. Certainly he would not have phrased it this way, for to his mind he had simply recovered the biblical conversion system, what he called the "Ancient Gospel." For Campbell conversion involved no dramatic experience but only a simple and straightfoward intellectual concession to the Gospel "facts." The simplest way to describe Campbell's argument is to say that he called disgruntled believers to turn away from the interior, subjective dispositions toward the outward, objective facts of Scripture.[2]

More specifically, Campbell described conversion in Lockean terms. Just as for Locke one learns by receiving outside data into a passive mind that categorizes that data, so also for Campbell one is converted by hearing the "facts" of the Gospel and accepting them as truth. Campbell claimed that there is no subjective experience to rely upon because God does not need to work that way. God has given us our five senses to receive the factual revelation in Scripture and this channel of truth is sufficient. In fact, for Campbell and other Christian Lockeans, subjective experiences can never be relied upon because they assume that the mind is capable of producing thoughts or emotions apart from the senses. One cannot experience God in this direct manner because these "experiences" lie outside the realm of the five senses and thus are illusory. Perhaps the most important consequence of this synthesis of Locke's philosophy and Christianity is that God cannot be experienced directly, but only through the agency of the senses—particularly seeing or hearing the words of the Bible.

Since this book focuses mainly on the damage this system has inflicted upon Churches of Christ, let us pause briefly to consider its advantages. The chief advantage is that it rescued those who were excluded from the revivalistic impulse. Those Christians who felt inferior in faith because they never achieved an earth-shattering experience to confirm their faith found a word of grace in Campbell's system. Now no one could second guess the authenticity of her own faith—if she agreed with the facts of Scripture and performed the commanded acts of obedience (repentance, confession and baptism) then she was a Christian. Moreover, she was a Christian to the same degree as anyone else who has done what she has. This system precluded the possibility that Christians could be ranked according to their ostensible "encounters" with God. Apart from the consequences of Campbell's thought, this was a brilliant argument presented at the right time and in the right context for many hurting believers.[3] There is however a very large downside.

3) The Problem with the "Dirt Philosophy"

There can be no argument with the fact that Campbell introduced sensualistic materialism into the movement, though there has been some argument over the degree to which Campbell and the movement were invested in this philosophy. Whatever the case, it is our contention that in the generations subsequent to Campbell the philosophy crept deeper into the consciousness of the movement. This progression or evolution of thought is quite natural, but we will need to explain the theory before displaying the facts that support it.

Among the many levels on which the human mind functions are two primary levels: cognitive and precognitive. Our cognitive thoughts are those we can separate, discuss and alter as we see fit. They are explicit thoughts. Others however are precognitive, that is, they are the thoughts or systems of thought on which we depend albeit unconsciously. Our precognitive thoughts are the thoughts and assumptions that are below the threshold of our own awareness. We do not realize we possess them until someone else reveals them to us. When they are brought into light we typically become very defensive about them because they have, without us knowing it, become essential to our thinking. Usually we either deny their existence or claim that they exist but are nonetheless valid. But most often we have difficulty coming to terms with them at all because we are unable to articulate them intelligibly.

The line between the cognitive and precognitive forms of thought is blurred by a rather large "gray area." This blurriness results from the fact that ideas evolve through time. What may have been a cognitive thought in one generation becomes located in the gray area for the next and may even become buried in the precognitive side in the following generations. This is a natural result of tradition. As ideas are passed through generations some are no longer explicitly passed along but assumed or gained through habit. What once may have been an overt idea—intelligible, able to be discussed and altered if needed—later becomes hidden; it still functions powerfully but at a precognitive level.

This evolution from idea to ideology is what occurred in the movement with Locke's philosophy. Campbell, at least according to Richardson, consciously employed sensualistic materialism as an argument against the neurosis created by revivalism. His followers in later generations, however, inherited the same philosophy but without the ability to discern its influence and relevance. They ceased viewing it as a response to revivalism and saw it (as Campbell himself began to) as part and parcel of biblical Christianity itself. As a result, many members of the tradition today possess a form of Locke's philosophy as a functional ideology who have never even heard the name of John Locke.

More importantly, the philosophy has become sacrosanct for many (as indeed it did for Campbell and Fanning). Rather than being a vehicle for passing on the biblical faith, it has been confused and intermingled with the biblical faith itself. Therefore when one attacks a tenet of this philosophy the attack is (mis)interpreted as an attack on the biblical faith itself.

Now, finally, we can understand where the two primary participants in the debate stood. Fanning was a second generation reformer. He had accepted Locke's philosophy, somewhat consciously, but was unable to deal with any attack upon that philosophy without misconstruing it as an attack on the biblical faith. Moreover, Fanning was unable to deal in a rational way with his dependence on this philosophy.

Consider this example. When Richardson exposed the intermingling of Locke's philosophy with the Christian faith, Fanning first replied that Locke was not a philosopher. If Locke was not a philosopher, according to Fanning, then there was no intermingling to discuss. Later, he changes his line of reasoning—indeed, he changes it about three or four times. He claims that he is not a "disciple" of John Locke, then swiftly defends Locke against the supposed misinterpretations of Richardson, and finally claims that at least Locke was a Christian philosopher. The double-mindedness and incoherence of Fanning's defense of Locke reveals a fact of great importance: this philosophy is becoming precognitive and ideological for Fanning.

On the other side of the debate, it is this uncritical acceptance of Locke that prompts Richardson to write his series of articles, "Faith versus Philosophy." Richardson portrays Locke's philosophy as a cancer on the movement that is sapping its Spiritual vitality. More than this, its progression into the recesses of precognitive thought is creating a situation in which it can no longer be discussed in a calm and critical manner. This is troubling to Richardson, who was committed to the movement but disturbed by the signs he perceived of a Spiritless future for Churches of Christ. The intensely personal nature of Richardson's struggle can be seen in this passionate plea:

> I do not then charge them [Fanning and company] with materialism on this question, as with an absolute vacuum. I do not allege that they have a bad meaning, but that they have no settled meaning at all. They do not understand themselves, nor the empty philosophy which they have unwittingly embraced under the guise of religion, which insidiously directs their religious thought, and like a demon beneath the veil of an angel, mocks at all their endeavors to make spiritual progress.

4) The Exploitation of the "Dirt Philosophy"

Now we are ready to discuss Richardson's actual problem with the Lockean philosophy. Actually, his problem was not with the Lockean philosophy *per se*, but rather with its rigid application to the whole of Christian existence. He agrees with Campbell that it was a good argument to lighten the burden of the revivals on weary, discouraged believers; but now, according to Richardson, the movement needs to complete its work of restoration. Campbell and his generation were relatively successful in restoring the centrality of the Bible to Christian life. And they did so using Locke's philosophy as a tool; but according to Richardson this was only the beginning and not the end of the restoration of New Testament Christianity.

Richardson used the metaphor of a temple to describe the situation facing the movement: "It is due to candor, however, to admit, that there are not wanting, earnest and thoughtful individuals who fear that the true temple of God has not yet been restored to these foundations; or that, if built, it has not, as yet, been filled with the Divine presence."[4] Campbell helped build the temple by restoring confidence in the words of the New Testament. Locke's philosophy aided Campbell in discerning the shape of Christianity by adhering closely and methodically to the actual words of the Bible. This method imparted to believers the necessary knowledge to restore the form and shape of the New Testament church. However, this same method (sensualistic materialism), Richardson argued, was now working to impede the ongoing task of restoration, for restoring the Bible to its proper place in Christian life is only the means to a much greater end: encountering the Divine Presence itself.

The "dirt philosophy" left no place for an encounter with God or for an actual sharing of the Divine Life, and this was the sum of its deficiencies for Richardson. A temple had been built by meticulously adhering to the measurements and dimensions set forth in the New Testament, but it was a temple with little room for the God who designed it. There is no Spirit in the temple. The words of Scripture echo and resound off the cold stone walls of a vacuous temple. This is because the philosophy of Locke has seduced prominent voices of the movement to stop at the words of the Bible. Only the words of Scripture apprehended through the five divinely created senses are needed for the fullness of Christian life according to these voices. Anything else is not only superfluous but skirts the hem of heresy.

Richardson claimed, in contrast, that the words and the Word are set forth with the aim of propelling Christians into a dynamic relationship with their author. We do not stop at the Word but proceed through the Word into the very heart of God who empowers us, through the Word, to live extraordinary lives. The words point to a strange new world; they compel us to travel there, and point out the illegitimate avenues to it. What they do not do, and must never do, is take the place of that world. When this happens one has committed a much greater travesty than misreading the words; one has misunderstood the very reason the words and the Word were revealed.

These claims may be rather modest by today's standards, and in truth they were modest in Richardson's time as well. This is the sharp irony of his life: it was not the truth for which he was contending that made him an outcast in the part of the movement that became Churches of Christ. In fact, Richardson had been writing about these very issues for years prior to 1857. Through all that time he remained a close friend and confidant to Campbell, was seen as a respectable leader in the movement, and was rarely attacked for his views by others in the movement. Why was he castigated on this occasion and not on others?

To answer this question we must go back to our discussion of cognitive and precognitive thinking. Recall our earlier statement that we are more defensive when our precognitive thoughts are exposed and critiqued because it is upon these that many of our beliefs and experiences depend. We are, without knowing it, heavily invested in these precognitive beliefs. We also claimed that Locke's philosophy was quickly becoming a precognitive belief for many in the movement at the time Richardson wrote his "Faith versus Philosophy" series. Add to this the fact that Richardson, modestly but unabashedly, attacked the synthesis of Locke and Christianity, and the furor provoked by Richardson begins to make sense.

Simply put, Richardson struck a central nerve in the movement. The system of thought created by Locke had become too closely tied to the more biblical principles of the movement to be critiqued in this way. Richardson's position was taboo because he attacked a system of thought that had become, or was perceived as, essential to the progress of the Restoration Movement.

Richardson's position was that the philosophy was not only separable from the tradition itself but was in fact harmful to it. Sensualistic materialism, he believed, would lead only to Spiritual lethargy and doctrinal foundering in the movement. He affirmed Campbell's desire to quell the excesses and exclusions of an overly-excited spiritualism, but he thought this could be accomplished without the aid of John Locke or any other philosopher. As we turn to some key themes in the debate, we will see why Richardson was unsettled by the corosive effects of the philosophy and how he hoped to lead his readers out of their Spiritual malaise into a fuller, more robust and balanced appreciation of God's activity in their lives.

Key Issues of Contention

We have been examining the underlying point of contention between Richardson and Fanning. Now we turn to examine how that underlying point surfaces in more explicit disagreements. As we examine these issues, keep two things in mind: Fanning's perspective on each of these falls squarely in line with Locke's philosophy, and Fanning's position and rhetoric will sound strikingly familiar to those who have grown up in Churches of Christ.

Faith

The word "faith" is used so widely and inaccurately by many today that it often yields little in the way of a central, clear meaning. Many of us tend to think just the opposite about this word: we think that most know exactly what the word means. Ask a five-year-old in Bible class about the meaning of faith and she will usually reply, without missing a beat, that it is believing that God is "up there." Most of us would probably give a similar answer without giving it much thought. According to the New Testament, both the kindergartner and many of us are wrong.

In the New Testament faith is not connected with the existence or non-existence of God. In other words, to believe in God did not mean to believe that God existed as one might believe that there is indeed life on Mars. Nor was God's existence the basis of faith; it simply was not an issue. First-century Christians did not encounter the thoroughly modern problem of atheism. The problem was not whether or not God existed but what sort of God was He.

Having said as much, it is much easier to say what faith is not than what faith is in the New Testament. Every New Testament writer had his own way of using the word: for Paul it was synonymous with trust and the proper response to the preached word; for John it was being in a right relationship with God and the entrance into a Divine communion; and for Matthew and Luke it was about following in the footsteps of Jesus. With all the different nuances of faith, however, one common denominator holds all the meanings together: faith is about a trusting participation in the Life of God. That is, faith is not an individual opinion, belief or theory, but an active, trust-full communion with God. To have faith is to be in a relationship (much like a marriage), and to lack faith is to second guess or mistrust the decisions of the Divine Partner. Paul talks about Christians taking part in the "faith of Christ" as we inherit the relationship Jesus had with the Father (Rom. 3:21-22; Phil. 3:8-9). This is the quintessence of faith.

Faith then by definition requires reciprocity—give and take by both the believer and the believed. This again presumes that the Life of God and the life of His disciples are connected in a direct way. This is where we would begin a discussion about the role of God's Spirit, but this is also the point where Fanning and his heirs would object.

Remember that for a strict Lockean, God cannot act directly on the individual heart or mind. This is because human minds are passive, unable to create ideas of themselves. Knowledge is limited to the five senses, and any knowledge that cannot be linked to what can be seen, heard, touched, smelled or tasted is illegitimate. This means that if God is to speak to us He must do so through the five senses and not directly to the heart. For a Lockean the human mind is simply not equipped with the receptors for any spiritual, non-sensible communication from God. We cannot be in a direct, personal relationship with God because we lack the senses to communicate with Him. God is spiritual and we can only know the physical. Therefore, God must always work through material vehicles and never directly; today the only vehicle for that working is God's written (visible or audible) Word.

This leads Locke to define faith as "the assent to any proposition not made out by the deductions of men, but upon the credit of the proposer as coming from God, in some extraordinary way of communication." More simply rendered, faith is the individual saying that a statement is true because it is attested to by a miracle. Therefore, when an individual reads Acts 2 and understands that after the miracle of Pentecost Peter proclaims "this Jesus whom you crucified is both Christ and Lord" and then decides that this is a true statement, he has placed his faith in God. He reads the statement and then agrees with it, thus he has faith. Faith therefore is simply a concession to the Gospel facts.

Fanning says as much in his fourth and fifth "Replies" to Richardson. He vaguely claims that faith does not end with the facts, but then quickly quotes, with a hearty endorsement, the above definition of faith given by Locke. For Fanning and many others, faith is little more than agreeing with the Bible. Obedience, or doing what the Bible says, is the next logical step, but it is separated from faith.[5] As we shall later note, this unbiblical separation between faith and obedience has caused untold amounts of grief for many Christians in Churches of Christ.

Notice carefully how this view subverts and denies the biblical notion of faith as a right relationship with God. This notion of faith has nothing to do with an active relationship; it is simply agreeing that God exists and that the New Testament is true. It is fundamentally no different than agreeing with the teachings of a good book, though to a much greater degree. It does not require or imply that the reader of Scripture has a relationship with the author of Scripture, but only that the reader concedes that what the book says about the author is (rationally) true.

This is precisely where Richardson poses a challenge to the Lockean synthesis of Christianity. He eloquently describes his more biblical, competing vision of faith by asserting:

> It [faith] does not terminate on the facts recorded, but these were recorded that our faith might reach forward to something else—to something which is not recorded; to something which could not be recorded; to something which passes wholly beyond this wretched objective philosophy under view, even to the power, the love, the personal and official character of our blessed Redeemer himself, realized

subjectively in the inner consciousness and affections of the soul.

Richardson was rightly disturbed by the lack of intimacy and participation between the believer and God under the Lockean conception of faith. Indeed, this vision lacks the vitality and Spirituality so evident in the New Testament conception of faith. It exchanges a Spirit-indwelt relationship with Jesus for a rather cold, rational acceptance of certain facts.

Richardson, to be sure, recognized the opposite dangers: faith certainly can become so dependent upon feelings and experiences that it disregards both the Bible and reason. Therefore, Richardson plotted what he believed to be a middle trajectory between an overly intellectualized faith and an overly experiential one. He agreed that our concession to the New Testament facts (e.g., Jesus is Lord) forms the "basis" of faith. These prompt and inform our belief, but our belief must never rest merely in these facts. Again, if we stop there, as did Fanning, then we miss the point of the words of Scripture: they are meant to launch us into an actual, personal relationship with God.

The facts must never simply be the terminus or goal of faith. The goal of faith lies within the Author of the words, not the words themselves. Faith never rests after having intellectually accepted the propositions of Scripture, but rests only in the very heart of God, which is precisely where those propositions direct us.

Now Richardson must account for the role of reason within faith. The Lockeans have safeguarded themselves against the possibility of their faith becoming overly subjective by embedding it in the objective ability of humanity to reason. They appeal to common sense: if it makes sense it must be true. So when Peter claims that Jesus is the Christ and Lord, this is true because it makes sense—how else could Peter speak in tongues if he were not telling the truth. For Fanning and the Lockeans reason brings us to the truth and faith accepts the truth as truth.

Richardson, standing in a long line of great Christian thinkers including Augustine, Anselm, Pascal and Kierkegaard, claims that the order is reversed. When one reads the Bible one discovers a world of thought and action that at first seems irrational. How is it that one becomes great by becoming a servant of all? How is it that the Son of God and Savior of the World can be born in an animal manger? And the greatest riddle to reason, how can Jesus' death on a cross be thought of as his glorification?

These truths seem irrational, but when one accepts them as the basis of faith, as faith grows closer to its terminus (a living relationship with God Himself), a certain way of reasoning develops from this faith. Before faith, the rationality that protests against these facts seems indisputable. But after faith, reason is perfected and these facts increasingly "make sense" from a Divine perspective. The cycle for Richardson is thus that faith introduces us to a strange truth that begins to make more sense as our faith grows. Reason follows faith and flows from faith, rather than reason fortifying and eventually creating faith. God does not have to meet the standards of human rationality to be worthy of our belief, rather God meets us as someone who deserves our trust and then shapes our reason to His way of doing things.

Now we can see more accurately the two versions of faith presented. The one rests upon reason and finds its home in the words of Scripture. We believe in, or more accurately, intellectually accept the words of Scripture and consciously decide to obey them to the best of our ability. The other version compels us to accept the words of Scripture but to follow those words into the heart of the mysterious One who speaks them. There, in that relationship, faith finds its rest, and the believer is sent into the world empowered by the Author of Life to live out the reality of faith for all to see.

Now ask, which version resonates in the worship of Churches of Christ? Which version have we heard preached, which version have we seen lived out and which have we inherited?

These two conceptions of faith ripple outward to other areas of Christian teaching and practice. We turn now to the implications of these two visions, most of which we have already anticipated.

The Spirit and the Word

Unlike the discussion on faith, many of us may feel as though we are on more familiar ground here, especially if we were to head this section "the Spirit versus the Word." Indeed, the discussion has traditionally been framed to set these two essential tenets of the Christian faith in opposition. The temptation that follows is to dissolve the one into the other. Of course the problem here is the way the issue is framed, not the issue itself. And again, the framing of the issue is due, in large part, to the Lockean premises embedded in the tradition of Churches of Christ.

Fanning, you will recall, was negatively impacted by his dealings with Jesse B. Ferguson. Ferguson professed a Spiritual Christianity which involved, among other things, mysticism, channeling dead spirits and a reckless disregard for Scriptural authority. It was perhaps Fanning's experience with Ferguson that strengthened the Lockean impulse within him. From Fanning's perspective, Locke's epistemology (theory of knowledge) provided an unshakable defense against this type of heresy and fortified the authority of Scripture.

Locke's philosophy provided this safeguard, positively, by emphasizing the importance of the written words of Scripture. Negatively, however, Locke's philosophy, when employed by Fanning and others, undermined any sense of God's indwelling Spirit. Recall our earlier discussion about the two sides of existence: the one accessible to the five senses (the phenomenal) and the other imperceptible (the noumenal). Lockeans emphasize the first half and overtly deny the second half. This can be seen in Fanning's own understanding of human nature. Human beings, he claimed, were not made to be "spiritual beings" but only "earthy" beings.[6] Our nature is earthy, only differentiated from animals by our ability to reason. Fanning concludes that we must not seek to go beyond our nature. We must abandon all talk of the spiritual side of nature.

This philosophy impacts Fanning's understanding of the Bible in that he is concerned not with what is beyond the literal page but only with what is visibly seen or audibly heard on the page. That is, one should not explore a Spiritual relationship with God but seek only to know and comprehend the actual words of Scripture. Again, the words and ideas presented in the Bible can be apprehended through the five senses, but the relationship to which the words point (according to Richardson) is beyond those senses. Therefore, just as any attempt to go beyond the senses is fraught with error, so also any attempt to go beyond the words is the surest path to heresy. When Fanning uses the word "spiritual" at all, he uses it only as a synonym for rational principles, not as demarcating another dimension of life where God relates to us.

Before proceeding we must make an important distinction. As a tradition that is committed to upholding the integrity of Scripture, we must be careful not to diminish the claims it makes on our lives. We must be equally careful, however, not to impose claims that it does not make on our lives. As we shall see, this second error can be as damaging as the first error. In one sense we can agree with Fanning's statement, quoted earlier: we do not want to go beyond the words of Scripture in that we do not want to import ideas from philosophies and other sources beyond the Bible. However, where the Bible itself urges us to go beyond the words, to the meaning and experience of the words, it becomes incumbent upon us to do so. If we are to be a people of the Book, we must follow the direction to which the Book points.

This distinction can be seen in a simple change of prepositions. Fanning urges us to put our faith *in* the Bible. We do this when we accept the biblical claims for its inspiration. And when we do this we have restored faith *in* the Bible. But we must not stop here. Not only should we restore faith *in* the Bible, we must also seek to restore the faith *of* the Bible, that is, to recover the practices and experiences recorded in the Bible. Instead of simply recalling, memorizing and reciting the words of the Bible, we attempt to enter into the biblical narrative, to see the world as the apostles saw it, to experience the Divine presence as at Pentecost, to undergo transformations like Paul underwent on the Damascus road, and to know the joy of Christ's disciples as He was raised from the dead. We seek, in short, to recreate the world of the Bible in our present lives, but in and of ourselves we cannot.

Here is where Richardson helps us. Fanning posed two alternatives: the Bible or the Spirit. He then dissolves the Spirit into the Word by claiming that the Spirit does not work apart from the Word. Framing the issue in this way presupposes a Lockean perspective, placing the visible and the invisible worlds at odds with one another. One must chose, according to Fanning and Locke, between what can be seen and what cannot be seen, between audible facts and a Spiritual relationship.

In contrast, Richardson claims that the two sides of existence, the physical (sensible) and the spiritual, are meant to work together. The words of Scripture are essential because they tell us who God is. But there is a vast difference between knowing who God is and knowing God (as in a relationship). We learn of God in the words, we get to know God through the words. The sensible words, when understood, lead into a deeply personal relationship with God made possible by the Spirit.

The Spirit makes the words of the Bible a reality in our lives according to Richardson. He makes the story of Jesus our story by recreating His faith in our lives. Both the Word and the Spirit are essential in this process. Without the Word we do not know who God is, but without the Spirit we do not know God as a living Presence in our lives. We need not pit these two realities against one another as Fanning does or emphasize one over the other as Locke does; we simply need to let each do its work on our minds and hearts. When we allow this to happen, our lives, worship and hearts can be conformed to the world of the Bible.

In ourselves we are incapable of performing the great task of bringing our own life narrative into the narrative of Scripture; only the Spirit of God, overseeing and controlling the process, can perform this work. Just as Paul, in Galatians 1 and 2, looks back at his own narrative and sees that narrative connected to the narrative of the Church and finally to the narrative of Christ Himself, so also we allow God's Spirit to reveal how we live out the narrative of Christianity in our lives.

Christian Life, Worship and Devotion

At this point we will leave the issues that were directly treated in the actual debate and venture to trace some implications of each vision. Though this section is brief it is perhaps the most important for two reasons. First, these issues deal with Christian practice instead of Christian theology. The different thought worlds we have endeavored to describe must ultimately be judged by the criterion of practice. More specifically, what sort of practice and character does each vision create? Second, these issues are more immediate to us. Having a well-informed theology is important, but its importance is secondary to one's character, worship and prayer life. It is our conviction that key aspects of Richardson's theology need recovery at this time primarily because they can enhance our way of living, worshiping and praying.

One of the most important doctrines of the New Testament is the doctrine of sanctification or Christian growth. One's devotion to Christ is measured not so much by where one is in one's walk of faith, but whether one is progressing, digressing or standing motionless. Fanning's Christian Lockeanism, with its preoccupation with the passive intellect and the words of Scripture, has fostered a distorted image of Christian growth. Because we are severed from Divine immediacy or the indwelling Spirit, Christian growth is often pictured in two inadequate ways.

The first way is that Christian growth is equated with one's knowledge of the Scriptures. If one's measure of faith is directly proportionate to one's knowledge of Scripture (as we saw earlier with Campbell), Christian growth becomes simply a matter of reading, learning and memorizing Scripture. Certainly becoming familiar with the Bible is vital to a healthy Christian existence, but simply knowing the words of the Bible with our minds does not produce faith and virtue. In fact, as most of us can testify, without other essential components of Christian growth, it can produce the vice of pride. The number of Christian leaders and biblical scholars who have fallen into depravity in their private lives serves as witness to the fact that virtue cannot be measured simply by what one knows.

The second inadequate way is a works righteousness mentality. If God cannot work personally in our lives but only through the Bible and the five senses, Christians are left to live out an impossible ethic without the Spirit's empowerment. In other words, Christians cannot expect the Divine assistance essential to living out the Sermon on the Mount, but must by their own power seek to meet the rigorous demands of the Gospel. The system devised by Campbell and expanded upon by Fanning and others separates belief in the facts of the New Testament and obedience to those facts. God has given the facts, we accept them, and then we are supposed to comply. The problem is that sanctification is too far removed from faith. Instead of faith opening us up to God's Presence in our lives which equips us to live out the New Testament ethic, we are left to our own devices to obey His demands—and with a small margin of error.

A well-rounded practice of worship also suffers under Fanning's theology. The central event becomes the preaching of the Word, where biblical data is imposed on our passive intellects. Worship loses the sense of an active communion of saints and angels; it becomes basically the place where the words (not so much the story) are recited, clarified and reinforced. The role of the congregation is to observe and listen, but not to take part in or be swept away by the all-consuming Presence of God. Again, we are severed from that Presence because of the heightened emphasis placed on the passive intellect.

The issue of prayer and devotion is an especially interesting point in this version of Christianity. Both Campbell and Fanning were baffled as to how to give a satisfactory answer to the simple question, "Why do Christians pray?" If the sole locus of God's presence is in the words of Scripture and if we have no real, personal relationship, then why ask God to heal, forgive and strengthen? The fact is, under Locke's philosophy, prayer and devotion (aside from reading the Bible) has little place in the Christian life. If God can work only through limited channels, and the primary channel is Scripture, we are left without the need for prayer. If we do invoke God's healing power, we almost by instinct continue to ask that God work through certain channels such as modern medicine ("guide the doctor's hands"). Though both Fanning and Campbell were men of prayer, their theology leads to perfunctory prayers and limits devotion to the intellect.

On the other side, Richardson's propelling fear was that the movement was becoming stale, lifeless and contentious under the practical implications of Locke's philosophy. In one of his first addresses in the debate, he clearly stated that the problem with the Restoration Movement was not so much its theology as its practice. He further believed that the root of the problem with its practice reached back to Locke.

If the key words for Fanning's vision are passive reception, then the key words for Richardson's vision would be dynamic participation. As faith grows in proportion to God's Presence emerging in our lives, so also sanctification is the process of our lives being further indwelt by God's Spirit. We do not grow in proportion to how much we know, but we know in proportion to how much God gives us growth. Our participation in His Life is the source for both growth and knowledge. We are not left adrift from His Life, but His Life flows into ours, thereby empowering us to live extraordinary lives. The impossible becomes possible because He wills it in our lives. God is the source and goal of our good works and He gives us the power to perform them. More than this, His character becomes our character, His nature becomes our nature, His Life becomes our life as we immerse ourselves in His Presence.

We believe that we have yet to see the "style" of worship that follows from a more dynamic and relational theology. We are confident that the congregation would cease to be observers and become full participants. Church would become communion; not just communion in the Lord's Supper but communion in song, communion in the preached word and communion in prayer. Every individual would be responsible for utilizing his or her gifts on behalf of the whole congregation and each individual would be the beneficiary of his or her neighbor's gift. It would be the pinnacle of our weekly worship, where God and a group of His people meet together in a radiant communion with unveiled faces. All would participate in one another's lives and in the very Life of God.

Finally, under Richardson's view, prayer and devotion would be a matter of "practicing the Presence." Prayer would assume a more pivotal and primary place in the Christian life. We would not pray simply because we are commanded to but because we are allowed to. Through this discipline our eyes would be opened to possibilities that we cannot even envision now. We would see God's actions in people's lives more clearly and distinctly than we ever thought possible because our prayers would increase our faith, our faith would increase our vision. As God's Presence became an everyday reality for us, we would sense His actions more deeply and personally.

Conclusion

For these changes to come about we must embrace a new vision of the Christian life, of God and even our own human nature. The crossroad of 1857 represented an opportunity for the Stone-Campbell tradition to take hold of a bolder, fuller and more vibrant vision of life in Christ. Richardson represented that vision, and he represented it in sharp defiance of a more anemic and stale vision of that life. Richardson's fear was that later generations would reap the leanness that the Lockean vision of Christianity imposed upon them. And we have. Many in later generations, to be sure, sought a more robust and meaningful relationship with God, but because of their ideas have either been without the language to describe it or have actually been blocked from such a relationship. The path that Richardson represented was in large part eclipsed by a more dominant path that lacked the theological language to account for God's work in the lives of His people.

Today Churches of Christ as a tradition stand again at a crossroad, a crossroad that is in many ways forced upon us by the crisis of our times. We will describe this crossroad in the next chapter. What interests us about this crossroad is that it makes the path Richardson represented—the rejected or side path—much more inviting to many of us. There is a reason for this: the Lockean philosophy of Campbell, Fanning and the many later reformers who pressed it into service unconsciously is being abandoned in our time. The dominant path of the tradition has been characterized not only by a reverence for Scripture but also by the philosophy of modernity.

Because many are now questioning the value of that philosophy, the tradition is afforded the opportunity once again to re-examine its commitment to modern philosophy. The crossroad at which we stand is similar in this respect to the crossroad of 1857. The question is almost identical: do we wish to remain invested in a philosophy that may actually undermine the goals of a full restoration of Christianity or do we wish now to abandon that philosophy?

The rest of this book is an attempt to answer that question. In Part II we will define the present crossroad and argue for an abandonment of the modern themes that have taken root. In Part III we will describe more positively the shape and direction of an alternate path. In this process we will have opportunities to revisit Richardson's vision; but just as he constructed his vision against the background of his own time, so also we will attempt to do the same in ours. His vision gives us the opening to describe a more expansive and vibrant vision, but we are not simply attempting to repeat his vision. We are nonetheless indebted to him. His voice, his quest for a more meaningful experience of God, stands as a beacon in our tradition. Its light inspires much of what we will have to say in the following pages.

Notes

1. See Thomas H. Olbricht, "The Rationalism of the Restoration," *Restoration Quarterly* 11 (1968), 77-88; Samuel L. Pearson, "Faith and Reason in Disciples Theology," in *Classic Themes of Disciples Theology*, ed. Kenneth Lawrence (Ft. Worth, TX: Texas Christian University, 1986), 101-29; and C. Leonard Allen, "Baconianism and the Bible among the Disciples of Christ," *Church History* 55 (March 1986), 65-80.

2. See D. Newell Williams, "The Gospel as the Power of God to Salvation: Alexander Campbell and Experimental Religion," in *Lectures in Honor of the Alexander Campbell Bicentennial, 1788-1988* (Nashville: Disciples of Christ Historical Society, 1988), 127-48.

3. See Leonard Allen, "The Comfort of the Gospel," in *Distant Voices: Discovering a Forgotten Past for a Changing Church* (Abilene, TX: ACU, 1993), 32-38

4. Richardson, "Faith versus Philosophy—No. 1," *Millennial Harbinger* 4th ser. 7 (1857), 135.

5. Fanning, "Fourth Reply to Professor Richardson," *Gospel Advocate* 3 (1857), and "Fifth Reply to Professor Fanning," ibid.

6. Fanning, "Fifth Reply to Professor Robert Richardson," ibid., 309.

Part II

At the Crossroads Again, 2001-

The quest for intimacy is the chief demand of a postmodern world. Centuries of autonomy, self-reliance and disbelief have left citizens of the Western world cold and isolated. Now, in droves, Western people are seeking greater intimacy with forces beyond human manipulation.

The specific question for the Stone-Campbell tradition is: Does it have the resources to create and sustain meaningful intimacy? Does it have the capabilities to satisfy the longings for a personal encounter with God?

4

Returning to the Road Not Taken

In order to understand the crossroad we stand at in Churches of Christ, we must understand something about the age in which we live. Indeed, the primary reason that we can speak of a crossroad or an alternative path for Churches of Christ is because of certain shifts that have taken place in the late twentieth century. The alternative vision of Robert Richardson (which is actually only alternative to some anemic and aberrant versions of Restorationism) is compelling because of the shifts in our age.

We live in an age unparalleled in history. Never in history has an era been this tumultuous, this rapid, this unstable and this open to the myriad of possibilities within its grasp. Technology has made us optimistic but distracted, progress has made us expectant but restless, and increased knowledge and awareness have made us intelligent but cynical. The future is wide open, which leaves room for the possibility of never before dreamed heights and never before envisioned chaos. Hope and fear are the two most prevalent emotions in our day spawned by our wearied motto "Change!" When all is analyzed, critiqued and summarized, one word remains as defining this age: uncertainty.

How did we get here, and more relevantly, how are we to flourish as Christians in a world such as ours? The first question may be answered with some precision while the second is more elusive and will occupy the bulk of the succeeding chapters.

The Crisis of Our Time

Many philosophers, sociologists and historians have used the word "postmodern" to describe our age. Its definition is as vague as the age it seeks to describe. Taken at face value, it simply describes the era that follows modernity but says nothing positively about this era. Let us then, in hopes of gaining some clarity about our age, describe modernity and we will then be better equipped to describe postmodernity and especially its effects on Churches of Christ.

The Rise and Fall of Modernity

History can be divided, (very) roughly, into four eras: the classical (the age of the Greeks, Romans and early Christians), the medieval, the modern and the postmodern eras. Our focus here is on the modern age because, according to many, it is the age out of which we are presently emerging. To understand our age as postmodern, as what follows the modern age, we must first understand what the modern age was about. The modern age, or modernity, encompasses the Enlightenment (beginning in the seventeenth century) and its aftermath in the eighteenth, nineteenth and twentieth centuries. This era is characterized by the great awakening of scientific knowledge inaugurated by Copernicus' theory that the sun and not the earth is the center of the universe.

As typically occurs, one field of study (science) effects many other fields. And so with the scientific advancements of the late sixteenth and early seventeenth centuries came tremendous shifts in philosophy and society in general. Borrowing from Diogenes Allen, we can see these shifts in the shape of four pillars of modernity.[1]

The first pillar of modernity is the unquestioned trust placed in human reason. Reason in this age supersedes all other sources of authority as the bar of judgment. Whereas before, the authority of the Church, the state and, in Protestant circles, the Bible determined how one lived, now each idea, each thought and each action must be judged according to its rationality. Rationality itself flows from knowledge, and knowledge was believed to be intrinsically good. Accruing knowledge increased one's skill in reasoning and thereby gave one greater direction in how best to live in the world.

Rationality however is incomplete without its counterpart and our second pillar, autonomy. Human autonomy literally means "self-rule" or "I rule myself" and often stands behind our usage of such words as independence. The French philosopher Rene Descartes proclaimed, "I think, [therefore] I am," and by so doing created a new definition of what it meant to be a self. The individual who thinks (reasons) is a self and since we all think we are all individual selves. More particularly, since we all think differently we are all isolated selves, each with his or her own definition of what is rational, what is right and what is worthy of belief.[2] Unlike before, the self is not gained through communion with God or fellowship with others, but is now defined by itself through its own ability to reason. The self is now thought to be self-sufficient. We will have much to say about this pillar in the chapters to follow.

The third and fourth pillars are in some ways effects of the first two, but also lay the foundation of modernity. The third is the belief in inevitable progress. Optimism ran rampant and unchecked through the age of the Enlightenment and modernity. With increased knowledge came increased arrogance concerning the possibilities of what humans, standing on their own two feet in subtle defiance of their Creator, could achieve. Indeed, the signs of inevitable progress seemed to be showing: new medicines were found to cure the sick, new elements were discovered to explain the phenomena of life, and modern culture itself seemed to be growing more sophisticated and triumphant than preceding cultures. The possibilities of our growth in knowledge and the assumption that knowledge is inherently good prognosticated a future of limitless potential.

The fourth pillar of modernity, which again took root in science and blossomed in the fields of philosophy and theology, is the notion that God is no longer necessary in scientific endeavors. In other words, whereas in previous times belief in God was the foundation for scientific inquiry, now God's existence or non-existence has nothing to do with such inquiries. The idea of God causing a sunrise, an apple to fall from a tree or planets to rotate is replaced by scientific laws explaining the earth's rotation, the laws of gravity and the movement of heavenly bodies. In other areas as well, such as in American politics, a sort of practical atheism is confused with neutrality—the compulsory bracketing of any beliefs about God in public discourse is a distant reflection of the original scientific dream of faith-free research.

It is difficult to overstate the practical effect of this move. Many have noted the result: theologians and Christian philosophers were left with a "god of the gaps." That is, whatever science could not explain was explained with reference to God, but as science discovered new laws and postulated new theories God was increasingly pushed toward the unexplored gaps of science. A famous dialogue between Napoleon and one of his scientists serves as an excellent example of this mentality. After explaining his new scientific theory to Napoleon, Napoleon paused with some concern and asked his scientist how God fit into this scheme. In reply, the young scientist simply said, "I have no need of that hypothesis."

Likewise, modernity spoke these arrogant and profane words to the source of all existence in the thought world it created. In a strikingly profound analogy, Middleton and Walsh compare modernity to the Tower of Babel in Genesis.[3] Much as the architects of that ancient tower sought to reach the heavens, thereby assuming God's position as sovereign, so also the architects of modernity sought to debunk God through an irreverent thirst for (godless) knowledge. "We have freed ourselves from our self-imposed tutelage," cried Immanuel Kant in the eighteenth century without calculating the risks of replacing God's authority with reason, autonomy and knowledge. Indeed, they had freed themselves from one sort of tutelage, but they left the ages that followed without a shelter from the crumbling of the tower they had constructed.

The Emergence of Postmodernity

Postmodernity is what follows modernity, and what follows modernity initially may best be described as crisis. The simple belief in God is unacceptable because such a belief in and of itself is not rationally justified. Finding refuge in one's community is not acceptable because the self is autonomous, unfettered by relationships. As for optimism, the inherent goodness of knowledge and inevitable progress—these notions seem tragically quaint after the depression, the invention and use of the A-bomb, the bloody results of Vietnam, and a new generation that has lost touch with meaning and purpose altogether. At some point reason and autonomy turned on themselves and now they have turned on us. They revealed to us that evil can result just as easily and much more efficiently from knowledge as from ignorance, and they left us very lonely in the process. And yet many believe that we have yet to feel the real aftershocks of modernity.

In an excellent essay Diogenes Allen joyfully anticipates the potential for theology and philosophy to rediscover God in this age, but he concludes sharply. He claims that these advances among the intellectuals may be for naught, because on a very practical level we are ripe for a widespread social catastrophe.[4] We have lost touch with ourselves, and in the process we have lost touch with our neighbors and God as well, and now we are left with very little to build upon. On one level many have turned to violence and revenge for an answer—as we can see any day of the week on the news; others to contemplative despair—as we see in the pop culture of our times; and of course there are always those who use their despair as a pretext for self-aggrandizement—as we see in the politicians of our time. These are precarious times and social chaos does indeed seem imminent, but this is not the end of the story: for these dry bones might live.

Christianity in Postmodern Times

We described postmodernity as crisis, but in doing so we were drawing not on contemporary usage of the term but on a very old understanding. Crisis derives from the Greek term *krisis* which meant the urgent need for decision. Often through hardships, trials or bleak revelations about the truth of one's status, an individual is forced into making a life-changing decision. The gauntlet has been thrown down and judgment (another definition of *krisis*) requires an immediate decision.[5]

This idea of *krisis* also happens to be very biblical, as is seen most readily in the Gospel of John. *Krisis* in John brings together revelation, self-judgment and decision. Underlying all of this was the fact that people could not confront Jesus passively—they left his presence changed for the better or the worse, but always changed. *Krisis* is John's way of describing this life-altering experience of meeting Jesus. More precisely, it described the moment that reveals where those who heard Jesus actually stood in relation to God. This moment of revelation was also a moment of judgment because the attitudes of the people about Jesus' ministry, brought to the fore by their interaction with Jesus, indicated God's judgment of those people. From this experience they had to make a decision in light of the revelation and encounter. Hence this moment of revelation also called for repentance, a renewed outlook on life or an outright rejection of Jesus and the God whom he revealed.

This rejection often took the form of individuals deceiving themselves into believing that nothing extraordinary happened in their meeting with Jesus. They convinced themselves that it was not God's activity that brought them to *krisis*, indeed that there was no *krisis*, but only that they had met with a self-deluded and dangerous demagogue. Jesus makes it clear however that by dismissing the experience, by denying the full weight of what happened, they served as their own judges. (For examples and fuller descriptions of this see John 3:16-21; 12:44-50.)

In John 3 Jesus faces a respected teacher of Israel, Nicodemus, who approaches him at night (presumably so that he can remain hidden from his peers). After baffling Nicodemus by the suggestion that he must be born again, Jesus explains that this is a moment of *krisis* for Nicodemus. Light has come into the world and this light seeks to make us radiant, but the world "loved darkness rather than light because their deeds were evil" (John 3:18-19). Jesus makes it very clear that it is not he who judges but rather the individual who judges himself in response to the situation. Nicodemus becomes disoriented and possibly offended by Jesus' words, yet he knows that he cannot leave the presence of Jesus unchanged. He either must run to darkness and invoke judgment or embrace the light of Jesus' truth. Judgment must be rendered, and Nicodemus must decide on which side of that judgment he will fall.

We, like Nicodemus, are left disoriented. Initially, we are disoriented not so much by confronting Jesus as by these perplexing times. But examined through the eyes of faith we see that the twilight of the gods is upon us, we see our situation revealed, we see the aspirations of our modern age eclipsed. We, as a society, are in a moment of *krisis*—though many choose not to acknowledge the *krisis* or choose not to acknowledge it as coming from God. Nonetheless, whether from God or not, there is revelation, judgment and the demand for a decision in the circumstances we daily face in contemporary culture. The revelation and judgment demand a decision on our part. We have made ourselves lonely, we have cut ourselves off from the God who seeks to indwell us. More than this, we have arrogantly trusted in our own abilities to remedy the situation, and finally in defiance of God we, like Prometheus, have sought to steal fire from the heavens. When we open our eyes to the truth of this situation we find ourselves in a moment of *krisis*.

The postmodern crisis emerges from the revelation that we are not autonomous, that there is more to life than what can be rationally ascertained, and that if there is no God, as Dostoevsky wrote, than "everything is lawful." The crisis is worsened by the fact that even after this revelation, even after our full-hearted acceptance of the revelation, we remain ill-equipped to escape the hold of these idolatrous and false ideas. Ideas such as autonomy, though we recognize them as illusory, are so deeply interwoven into our culture and even into our own beliefs that we cannot fully break free of them. We live in a world where modernity, though it is crumbling, remains very powerful and will continue to wield power for some time. Worse still, we are all moderns, even those of us who do not wish to be (that is, those of us who are "recovering moderns").

A certain despair arises: we have been wrong, naive, rebellious and, quite frankly, ignorant about fundamental aspects of our very existence. The despair comes from the revelation of these facts about our age and from the fact that we are saturated in this age. From this point of view, we might define postmodernity as the recognition that modernity was faithless, wrong and designed to fail. We who like to call ourselves postmodern are those who recognize that, at least to an extent, we are mired in the failures of modernity. These failures—indeed our failures—confront us each day and they cut deeply. However, this laceration calls us into a decision that is laced with hope: do we desire to be healed or would we rather deny the crisis of our time?

Healed of what exactly? In a word, estrangement. Modernity has driven a wedge between us and God, us and our neighbors, and even us and ourselves. Cold reason may make us astute, but reason alone cannot comfort us in seasons of despair, nor can reason account for moments of indescribable elation. Modern thinkers would have us remain here, detached from such experiences, as would many postmodern theorists who fear there is no hope of healing. Such pessimism is captured by a philosopher who announced, after a lifetime of struggle with these issues, that "only a god can save us." He was not far from the truth. God is, as He has always been, in the process of saving us.

A new breeze is blowing through the ashes of the crumbling tower. This breeze, while not fully definable, seems to whisper that we need not remain in this state. We need not remain torn or estranged from our relationships with God, others and ourselves. There is promise of a sanctuary from the collapsing tower of modernity, and reminder of some very basic yet forgotten truths: (1) The proof that sustains our faith in God comes not from our rational gropings but from the fruit of His Spirit blossoming in our lives; (2) our most basic human drives issue from the desire to love and be loved, not from the desire to be autonomous; and (3) we only know ourselves as individuals in the midst of relationships with others, not as "thing[s] which think."[6]

Estrangement is the condition to be faced in this age, and it is being faced, rightly or wrongly, in our present society through a renewed quest for intimacy. Many feel the deep-seated desire for greater intimacy with God, one another and their own selves. We see signs of this desire throughout the culture. They are as diffuse as common revival movements like Promise Keepers, to less spiritual and more ethnic movements such as the Million Man March, to bizarre and outlandish movements such as angel-mysticism and new-age crystal worshiping. Yet all of these movements, whether right or wrong, pious or irreverent, point to the same need we all feel at different levels: we desire a real, meaningful communion with God, each other and ourselves.

Now that we have some clarity about our present age as both modern and postmodern (as well as the stormy debate between these two tendencies within us), we have the proper perspective to return to the clash between Tolbert Fanning and Robert Richardson in 1857. We turn to it now, however, not to study its history but to study its future. For their debate, now a century and a half behind us, rages within our churches and within our own hearts.

Two Paths of the Tradition of Churches of Christ

Two somewhat contradictory effects of the collapse of modernity can be seen in our time: rampant individualism and the rediscovery of tradition. On every hand we hear sentiments such as these: "all authority rests squarely upon my own shoulders; I decide what is right and what is wrong for me; I chose my own path; I am not indebted to any tradition or to any other human being." Some have called this, ironically, the anti-tradition tradition. This anti-tradition tradition is as nonsensical as an entire culture proclaiming in unison, "I am unique!" and then failing to hear that each is only mimicking the voice of its culture—which is anything but unique. Despite its absurdity this cultural impulse is the last, dying breath of modernity.

The effects of individualism are catastrophic; it only creates further isolation, loneliness and eventually despair.

A Word on Tradition

Let us then turn briefly to the rediscovery of tradition. If we can somehow rid ourselves of the notion that tradition is a dirty word then we may look at it afresh. In order to do this, we must distinguish it from its unhealthy counterpart "traditionalism." Traditionalism allows a tradition (which may be good in and of itself) to confine and restrict the options of the present with the demands of the past. Traditionalism occurs when tradition becomes locked into one particular, historical mode and rigidly rejects all attempts to adjust to the present. It demands conformity rather than refreshment, adherence rather than revision and submission rather than creative participation. As the historian of Christian tradition Jaroslav Pelikan once wrote, "Tradition is the living faith of the dead; traditionalism is the dead faith of the living."[7]

Tradition itself is neither good nor bad, it simply is. Tradition is unavoidable. Whether we like to admit it or not, we are all part of traditions. Our task as responsible human beings is not a vain avoidance of tradition, but rather to identify ourselves with vibrant and healthy traditions. Obviously, we believe that the Restoration tradition can be such a tradition. We are firmly rooted in that tradition, and are seeking to dialogue with the historical voices that have shaped it.

This does not mean however that being part of a tradition requires extensive knowledge of the tradition. Members of Churches of Christ may not know who Alexander Campbell, Tolbert Fanning or Robert Richardson were, but, even so, are carrying on their tradition. We do so in our style of worship, our doctrines and even in our ways of thinking. In all of these things we are "communing with the dead," carrying on the tradition called the Stone-Campbell or Restoration Movement.

A healthy tradition allows room for revision, growth and even reconsideration. In a healthy tradition adherents may respectfully question some tenets, even some essential tenets, of its thought world. Indeed, a healthy tradition carries on a dialogue with enough flexibility to heed the voice of the outsider. To be sure, there is continuity—we must have some core beliefs that identify us with our predecessors—but there should also be room for a creative, growing edge around those core beliefs.

Here we approach a gray area, for who can draw with precision the lines of a tradition, much less the Stone-Campbell tradition? Who determines, and by what standard, who is outside the tradition and who is within it? These are the difficult questions confronting us at the present crossroad of the Stone-Campbell tradition. Such questions are forced upon us by the crisis of our age.

We can say with great certainty that the Stone-Campbell tradition has from the outset contained a quite diverse constituency. From its humble origins, the movement welcomed both the rationalistic "intelligentsia" such as Campbell, as well as the revivalistic "common folk" such as Barton Stone and many in his circle of influence. It embraced the "biblicist" southerners such as Fanning and David Lipscomb as well as the more spiritually-minded northerners such as Richardson. Certainly these various elements were often at odds with one another, but then again a good controversy waged in good faith is a good sign of a healthy tradition.

Unfortunately, our movement is now at a point where good controversies are not waged in good faith, indeed are often waged somewhere below the threshold of Christ-like respect for the opponent. Many have simply given up the task of holding the movement together through fruitful, if spirited, dialogue.

Yet there is a further, more serious sign that the tradition is losing some of its vibrancy. Put simply, we are quickly losing our shared identity as a tradition. In other words, inasmuch as a tradition defines who we are, many of us are losing a sense of ourselves. Some express this loss in the form of naively refusing to admit that they belong to any tradition; others express it by drawing on an overly propagandized version of the tradition; and still others express their loss with a premature concession that there is little within the tradition that makes it compelling to this age. These signs point not so much to fragmentation (though, without doubt, there is a great deal of fragmentation) but to a subtle kind of decay. To the extent that the tradition is showing signs of decay, we who belong to it are losing our very identity.

This of course begs the question: Is the tradition worth saving? Has the Stone-Campbell movement itself a place in the postmodern world or are we ourselves making it irrelevant by giving up on the task of traditioning—that is, bringing the tradition up to date in a way that maintains continuity with its past?

With this question we have come full circle, for answering questions about the vibrancy and future of the tradition depends on how it fares before the crisis of our times. If the tradition lacks the resources to address the (post)modern experience of estrangement, then it will likely continue in the process of decay, settling further into an isolating traditionalism. On the one hand, this tradition has traveled the path of modernity, autonomy and estrangement. On the other, some within it have tread a path that opposes modernity, a path with a fuller and less restrictive understanding of God's involvement in our world. The hope for continuing vibrancy rests in the ability of people in the tradition to reach back into the past and draw upon these latter resources, even at the risk of changing the present.

The Main Path of the Tradition

Meeting the demands of a postmodern world is far too broad for what we have in mind. In any cultural shift some demands are illegitimate for Christians to meet. These demands must of course be rejected—as they should have been when Western culture shifted to the modern worldview. Some of these demands however can provoke the recovery of essential parts of the Christian faith that we have neglected. In the Bible we read of God using individuals, such as Cyrus, who were not included among God's people to accomplish something on their behalf (see Isa. 44 and 45 for example). Other times God used people and governments who were unaware that they functioned as His instruments (Pharaoh, Judas, or the *Pax*

Romana in Romans 13 are examples). Throughout the Bible and into the present day God uses people, social movements and ideas that seem to have little to do with God's Kingdom in order to accomplish some specific purpose.

Likewise, God may be using many of the voices crying out in our postmodern world to remind us of those essential parts of our faith that we have neglected. My teachers in Canada like to call these voices "Cyrus figures." Certainly, when the world at large seeks greater intimacy with God and neighbor and turns to Eastern and syncretistic religions to fulfill that need, we should repent of our forgetfulness. It was in fact Jesus who issued the double love command and it was he who promised never to leave us. Somehow the world did not hear our message or somehow we neglected to live out our message or somehow we forgot our message.

The quest for intimacy is the chief demand of a postmodern world, and it is a demand that Christians should be able to meet. Centuries of autonomy, self-reliance and disbelief have left citizens of the Western world cold and isolated. Now, in droves, Western people are seeking greater intimacy with forces beyond human manipulation and beyond a life that has grown mundane. Not simply the world, but Christians also are seeking avenues through which they might encounter their Creator in a more direct and meaningful way. Thus the specific question for the Stone-Campbell tradition is: Do we have the resources within our tradition to create and sustain meaningful intimacy? Does it have the capabilities to satisfy the longings for a profound personal encounter with our God?

Many have said and are saying no. And their no has in large part been justified by the tradition. It cannot be denied that there are powerful voices in our background who will not allow these desires to be met. In fact, it may be argued that the main path of the Stone-Campbell tradition has found itself at odds with this desire, and for those who look only at this path there is little room for achieving the sort of intimacy of which Jesus himself spoke (John 15:4).

There is however a side path that can provide some of the theological resources to remain a part of the tradition while enjoying a fuller and more intimate relationship with Christ in our everyday lives. Pursuing it will mean creative and critical interaction with our tradition. Specifically it will entail walking down a side path that has been largely forgotten.

The main path of the tradition is very much at home within the confines of modernity. Recall from the last chapter Fanning's emphasis upon the "words and facts of scripture" and a "purely formal religion." Recall also that Campbell's system, adopted and sanctified by Fanning and subsequent leaders, was based upon data collected by the five senses which is then categorized and combined into complex ideas like God and other Christian doctrines. Much as a scientist gathers data from the environment, so also the Christian gleans discreet facts and precise instructions from the Bible.

This system of thought, which makes up the main path of the tradition, is a thoroughly modern theology that cannot meet the desire of our postmodern age for a deeper communion. More importantly, it denies the biblical role of God's Spirit. The primary reason this modern theology is faltering badly today is that it fails to take seriously the dynamic, Life-giving Presence of God in our lives. It has denied explicitly—and all too often continues to deny implicitly—that God can work within our hearts, that the Spirit can invigorate and give meaning to our practices, and that God is today building heavenly communities in our faith communities.

Why does it deny these things? What specifically does it contain that rules out a living, personal and communal relationship with God? Simply put, this system of thought contains an aberrant view of the self, an understanding that disallows or seriously diminishes God's role in the formation of who we are. Campbell and many others maintained a functional belief in God's involvement in our lives, but their assumptions made such beliefs difficult to sustain for later generations. Specifically, they assumed an understanding of the self that is built upon and inseparable from the autonomous self described by modern philosophers such as

Descartes and Locke. At the core of Campbell's system was the assumption that what defines us as human is our ability to collect and store data. This view of the self claims that our identity is founded upon our ability to rationally accumulate such data. It assumes that our reason defines us as human beings.

The underlying problem with such a notion is that the self stands aloof from the creative initiative of God in making us who we are and who we are to be. Hence, estrangement is built into this view of the self. Rather than God working in our lives, shaping our identities, revealing who we are in relation to who He is, we are seen as separate from God, as "thinking things" that are "self-ruled." The gap between our autonomous identities and God is closed only by our own rational efforts to collect and compile biblical information about God, ascending through our own reason and our own works to a God who is far removed from us. God Himself, according to the implications of autonomy, does very little to reach out to us.

In fact, if we are autonomous and made in God's image, then God must be supremely autonomous. It is a very small step from the illusion of human autonomy to the myth of Divine autonomy, to a picture of God sitting in Heaven alone occupied by contemplating Himself. In strong counterpoint, while we acknowledge that God's existence is not dependent on anything, we also assert that His nature is defined by love, not autonomy. If we take seriously and literally John's words, "God is love," than we must also understand that loving relationships are integral to God's very being. In other words, God's nature is to give Himself to the world, not to contemplate Himself in isolation from the world. We will return to these key points in subsequent chapters.

At its core, though few would state it so starkly, the autonomous self is left to its own devices to reason its way to God. Faith rests not in God's ability to make us who we are but in our own ability to find God in the pages of the Bible. This view of the self has left us distant from God, isolated from one another and estranged from what God designed us to be. Autonomy is an idea that enslaves us to our own reason. More importantly, autonomy isolates us. It insists that I alone am to plumb the biblical data for truth; I alone am to love my neighbor even though my neighbor is unable to contribute to my self-understanding; and I alone must live out the demands of the Gospel despite Jesus' words that without God's involvement in our lives such an attempt is futile (Matt. 19:25, 26).

In this way autonomy places an impossible burden on us. For those of us in the Stone-Campbell tradition, this is the crisis of the postmodern age. The assumptions about human autonomy and reason found in the writings of some of our greatest leaders are largely responsible for the way we experience this crisis. Their assumptions about autonomy have created an unnecessary distance between us and God. This is not to lay all the blame at their feet. Their insights and intuitions launched a lively tradition. But some of these very insights, contrary to their intentions, have had damaging effects as well. The modern philosophical assumptions that laced many of their biblical insights created the distance between us and God, not their insights themselves.

This distance is experienced in sharp and painful ways. Many feel lonely even in the midst of a communal worship of God. For others the words of Scripture feel less like good news than words of condemnation. Those words are not heard within the context of God's Presence with us and in us, but only as God's edicts issued from afar. For others the story of Jesus and the Apostolic Church feels distant, as if it is not our story but someone else's. For others the abundant Life that Jesus promises us in this life seems available only as a shadowy dream for the next life. And for still others, the experience of Pentecost seems utterly foreign, as if it was only their experience and not in some sense also our own.

Church members are responding in different ways to this situation. Some are leaving the tradition in search of a church home that can provide the intimacy for which they long. Others are resigned simply to accept a disquieting mediocrity surrounding their relationship with God. And others are laboring to achieve greater depths of intimacy in worship and life, but are doing so under the heavy feeling that they are defying the tradition. None of these options are necessary. It is possible for us to enjoy a fuller fellowship with God and one another while being faithful to the central tenets of the Restoration tradition. Indeed, as we shall argue (Chapter 6), these central tenets compel us to pursue a fuller fellowship with God and one another.

We can examine our tradition afresh and discover the riches of communion with God for which we long. It is possible and, we think, necessary to preserve the best parts of the tradition while laying aside the philosophical assumptions that have proven counterproductive to God's work in the present. We will find insight and encouragement in this effort by exploring the "less traveled" path.

The "Less Traveled" Path of the Tradition

The good news for those in the Stone-Campbell tradition seeking to steer a faithful course through the postmodern age is that there is a side path to our tradition. As we have seen, though there are jewels along the main path itself, valuable and important riches lie on the side path. The side path is comprised of voices that have not been readily heard. Many of these voices were muted by their contemporaries, marginalized by their adversaries and labeled heretics in the historiography of Churches of Christ. They have been treated this way, mainly, because they took issue with the cultural, modern background to the movement. Though they are often accused of misinterpreting the Bible, it is in fact a misinformed reading of the Bible against which they raised their protests.

This side path is somewhat difficult to trace. Indeed, we are not claiming that it is a cohesive, easily traceable path but only that there are tendencies that emerge in certain figures that taken as a whole comprise a discernible side path. Barton Stone's revivalism, David Lipscomb's apocalyptic worldview, and Richardson's understanding of the Spirit are examples. It is not that any of these figures were in total agreement, or if taken alone would necessarily agree with the vision we shall present. It is only that they, and others, possessed certain tendencies that anticipated somewhat the vision we shall set out for Churches of Christ in a postmodern world. Such individuals and such ideas are the resources that can give us a different, perhaps more hopeful, angle from which to view our present situation.

Actually our claim is not even that audacious since we are focusing on one primary figure—Robert Richardson. His theology of the Spirit directly addresses the crisis of our age and the crisis of our tradition. Yet Richardson, in his desire to foster a greater awareness of God's involvement in our lives and worship, is not alone. Throughout our history a cadre of others has echoed his sentiments, though their concerns were often met with resistance. Their path is neither so narrow as to permit only one lonely traveler nor so wide as to be dominant. This path was in fact a side path distinct from the more dominant path.

The key element that makes this side path compelling, indeed essential for the health of the Stone-Campbell movement in a postmodern age, is a more biblical understanding of the self. We have described the deviant, modern view of the self—the thinking self or the autonomous self—as a view that has left us isolated. This view of human nature insinuated itself into the movement and eventually characterized the dominant path. The less traveled path does not so much contain a rival view of the self as much as it assumes, points toward and allows room for a rival conception. Richardson does not write against autonomy directly, but his understanding of God's activity in our world clearly implies that he does not understand the self or God as autonomous. Likewise, the understanding of God's dynamic and personal activity in our lives found among most of those on the side path is simply too profound for the narrow confines of autonomy.

Later we will describe this conception of the self more fully, but we want at least to introduce it here. This rival view of the self is so intimately connected with our understanding of God that we cannot describe who we are without also describing who He is. This view, which we will call the relational self, is unlike the view of the autonomous self that understands human nature only in reference to the individual. The relational self, conversely, claims that we cannot even begin to understand who we are without first understanding our lives and God's Life as a deep, mysterious and intimate relationship. More precisely, a relational view of the self insists that our very being, our nature, is defined and sustained by our participation in God's Life. We do not make our selves into selves through our frail reason; rather God alone is the well-spring of our identity. We will develop this seemingly new, but actually very old, understanding of the self and of God in Chapter 6.

Some notion of the relational self, however under-developed, is evident in Richardson's theology of the Spirit (described in Chapter 2). An understanding of the self as deeply covenanted with God and fully dependent on God's Presence allows Richardson to set forth a more open, Spirit-indwelt and experiential approach to Christianity. The relational understanding of the self, implicit in Richardson's thought, allows him to create space for a richer, more personal involvement of God in our lives, allowing us to enjoy fresh visitations from His Spirit within the parameters of Scripture.

The relational self also serves as an essential corrective to the assumptions about human autonomy. Campbell's view that Scripture is basically an inspired collection of facts and Fanning's refusal to acknowledge God's personal involvement in our lives flow directly from their philosophical assumption that we are autonomous by nature. In contrast, Richardson's understanding of our world and our lives as permeated by God's creative and regenerative presence assumes a self that is relational. For us to recapture a consistent and expansive vision, however, we must go a bit deeper than Richardson went.

It is worth repeating that Campbell had good reason to turn to Locke (and the autonomous self) as an antidote to the neurosis of revivalism in his day. Campbell would not have endorsed our description of autonomy, but he did, contrary to his own intentions, assume a view that is very near our description. Like all of us Campbell was limited by the time in which he lived, restricted by the theoretical tools at his disposal and driven to remedy the specific problems of his day. There is no reason to doubt that Campbell had anything less than the noblest and most biblical of intentions, or to doubt that he actually recaptured some of the most basic and valuable biblical insights. Nonetheless, and also like the rest of us, he was blind to some of his own assumptions and their repercussions for later generations.

But we must also quickly note that today we are faced with a different sort of neurosis, one that results from an unnecessary distance placed between us and God. We believe that the latent potential of our tradition has yet to be realized. Further, we believe that the possibility of its flourishing in our day depends on our readiness to return to the less traveled path. For many of our communities gripped by the malaise of modernity, for many individuals alienated by the demands of autonomy, Richardson's less traveled path offers great promise for a more meaningful relationship with God within the Stone-Campbell tradition.

Richardson was a gifted theologian and an inspirational writer, but like Campbell and the rest of us he was also limited by the times in which he wrote and the people to whom he wrote. His path stands separate from the dominant path in the Stone-Campbell movement because he refused to domesticate the experience of the Spirit within the Lockean philosophy, not because he lays out a complete, well-rounded alternative to that dominant path. Our goal in this book is to point to Richardson's way as an alternate path, an under-developed counter vision, and to begin (in succeeding chapters) pointing toward a fuller, more expansive, more biblically adequate vision—one which seeks to recover the Divine Presence while at the same time avoiding the pitfalls of a reactionary, overly "subjective" and unbiblical experience of the Spirit.

Before describing this vision, we turn to examine some roadblocks that are particularly prominent in the main path of the tradition. We have hinted at these throughout but we are now prepared to view them more directly. These are the practical barriers on the dominant path of the tradition, barriers to a fuller and more intimate relationship with God. We begin with a story.

Facing the Roadblocks

My wife Holly sometimes tells of the summer several years ago when she went backpacking in the Colorado Rockies with a group of twelve novice backpackers. A group of teens from church had needed another adult sponsor for their trip. Holly had never been on a wilderness backpacking trip, and so she had naively said yes. For three months she had jogged and exercised trying to get her body in shape.

The trek began at Big Meadows Reservoir, elevation 9,000 feet. Her pack, stuffed with enough food and gear for a six-day trip, weighed about 30 pounds. Led by an experienced wilderness guide named Jim, they set out in early morning for the Continental Divide. The trail was almost all uphill. Switchback after switchback led to more upward climbs.

Hour after hour they walked. Bone-deep weariness began to set in. Unprepared muscles were assaulted and stretched to the limit. The novice backpackers more and more turned to their guide for hope and solace. "Don't you think it's just another half mile or so?" And "Do we get to go down hill soon?" Just when they thought they could not go another step, it began to rain. They pulled out their rust-orange ponchos and tried to stay dry. Soggy shoes and socks began to make sad, squishy noises.

Holly later said that the day's hike was the most exhausting, straining, humiliating experience of her life. "As my body deteriorated, my mind slowly began to grind down to its basest level," she remembered. "I wanted to scream and burst into tears, but I didn't want to become one of Jim's 'pathetic backpacker' stories."

Late in the afternoon, after being on the trail for eight hours, they arrived at the first day's campsite. They pitched their tents in the drizzle. Everything was damp—shoes, socks, clothing, hair. Not only was Holly physically exhausted but she was angry and frustrated. Her mind could think only of abandoning this crazy trip and getting back home. She crawled into her sleeping bag trying to get warm and trying to make it all go away. And except for a brief excursion for a supper of freeze-dried food, she stayed there all night.

The drizzle stopped around dark and some of the other hikers emerged from their tents to see if they could start a fire. They eventually rounded up enough dry wood to build a sizable blaze. They gathered around it and began to warm themselves, chattering and laughing. Several called out to Holly to come join them around the fire but she didn't. She wouldn't. She had created her own little igloo, and she stayed there, still damp, shivering, nursing her wounds, unable to sleep.

Holly could see the shadows of the others as they huddled around the fire and could hear their subdued joy as they moved in the circle of its warmth. The flames eventually burned down, and everyone—everyone except Holly—went to their tents warm and dry. But Holly never got warm and never went to sleep. Damp and cold and angry, she lay there all night, her mind concocting irrational plans to escape and get back home.

What barriers kept her from the fire that night?

What barriers keep us from God's Fire? What roadblocks keep us from the warmth and richness and delight of God's Life?

Rejection of Spiritual Experience

One enormous roadblock has been the constricted worldview that has characterized modern Western societies and that we have adopted without much conscious thought. Those who stand behind this barrier, we could say, do not believe in the Fire—or if they do, consider it now reduced to little more than smoldering embers. There are no bright Fires of Presence today. There is a creator God, natural laws, revealed truth. There are teachings, commands, moral rules, and we attempt to understand and obey them. We do the best we can. Through study we seek the "mind of Christ." But bright Fires of Presence belong to earlier times—the time of Abraham, the age of Moses, the era of Jesus and the apostles—not our time.

In the churches we attended while growing up, we received mixed messages. On the one hand, we often sang songs that spoke of a rich and personal communing with the Lord and that hinted that He might be up to something in our lives:

* Beyond the sacred page I seek Thee Lord;
    My spirit pants for Thee, O living word. . . .
* Revive us again, fill each heart with thy love,
    Let each soul be rekindled with fire from above.

But on the other hand, we got the distinct and strong message that the Lord had left us his written word or "plan" and that it was pretty much up to us to understand and obey it.[8]

Outside some of the songs, we did not gain much of a vocabulary for speaking of a personal relationship with God and of God doing something in our lives. We sang about seeking God "beyond the sacred page," but nobody ever described for us what that might be like. We sang about being "rekindled with fire from above," but since we did not hear anyone talking about that happening, we assumed it probably didn't. In fact, we talked negatively, sometimes even scornfully, of those who professed some personal experience with God. Such fires were suspect. They were dangerous fires to gather around. They burned too hot and too unpredictably, and easily became threatening wildfires.

The roots of this suspicion lie deep in the theological tradition of Churches of Christ. As we have already seen in Chapter 2 and 3, Alexander Campbell reacted strongly against the popular Christianity of his day with its stress on dramatic conversions. He was disgusted by the emotionalism he witnessed and read about in "revivals." He believed that feeling was overriding biblical fact and that disturbed him. Against these extremes he sought to minimize conversion and sanctification as "experiences" and to emphasize their intellectual, volitional character. This emphasis became even more stark and pronounced as the tradition hardened in the generations that followed. Yet such a stance is an aberration from classic Christian doctrine and practice. The classic Christian tradition has always, in its doctrine if not always in its practice, left room for personal experience of God.

Behind this sharp diminishment of Spiritual experience was a modern worldview. Worldview can be defined as the "culturally structured assumptions, values, and commitments underlying a people's perception of reality."[9] The birth of the modern worldview brought a deep-seated change in the way we perceive reality in the Western world. This new worldview was fundamentally materialistic and rationalistic, that is, it stressed the visible/physical and the supremacy of human reason. It steadily called into question the "supernatural" and the miraculous (including, among the more radical, the miracles in the Bible). Its standards of truth were scientific and "natural."

The modern, Western worldview has set deep within us a pervasive skepticism regarding spiritual and "supernatural" things. Very many of us, without even thinking about it, became functional deists.

Deism was a Christian heresy spawned in the late seventeenth and early eighteenth centuries by the rise of the new mechanistic worldview. Deists like John Toland (author of *Christianity Not Mysterious,* 1696) believed that God was the great creator/designer, that God set up fixed natural laws to govern the cosmos then left it to run according to those fixed laws. God had wound up the clock of the world so that it runs without further need for divine involvement. The conduct of life was thus left entirely to human beings and human reason.

Strict Deism was confined to a fairly small group of intellectuals in the eighteenth century. It soon receded as a movement. But its basic idea of the supremacy of uninterrupted natural law came to pervade modern thinking. This idea became a centerpiece of the modern scientific worldview.

In such an environment, the spiritual realm assumed by Jesus and Paul steadily has been thinned down. It has tended to seem unreal to us moderns. We are Christians of course—conservative and Bible-believing. We believe in God, Christ, an inspired Bible, ancient miracles, a future judgment. Probably a vague belief in angels. But a palpable spiritual realm has receded. The world of the here and now, of the measured and the managed, of scientific law, has overwhelmed us. Dallas Willard calls this condition "Bible Deism."[10]

We are conditioned against Divine Presence and interaction in our world. We do not expect it. We do not look for it or have eyes prepared to see it. We speak of "providence" but our providence is hardly distinguishable from good fortune or the favorable outworking of unbending natural laws. God's intervention, healing and deliverance can most always be explained away, attributed to natural forces, to coincidence or simply overlooked. Real personal encounter and communion with God seems strange for many, even heretical for some.

We say that we do not want to found our faith on experience but on divine revelation recorded in the Bible. That's good and proper. But in practice we tend to accept very little that does not fit with our mundane experience. In theory we are Bible-believing but in practice we reject much of what the Bible says about God's involvement in the world. We have not experienced Divine Presence and intervention (or at least have been unable to name it), so we readily conclude that God must no longer be present or intervene in that way—in spite of the fact that the Bible is replete with stories to the contrary.

The modern worldview has given us deeply ingrained and mostly unconscious habits of viewing reality. Even if we are Christians, these habits tend to be shaped to some degree by modern, secular assumptions. Indeed, we moderns have been immersed in an secular worldview. And these habits and assumptions are extremely difficult to dislodge or alter.

Our worldview determines, more than we know or usually admit, what we look for, what we are able to see, and what we find as we read and apply Scripture. Karl Barth once wrote that the question, "What is within the Bible? has a mortifying way of converting itself into the opposing question, Well, what are you looking for?" He added: "We shall always find in the Bible as much as we seek and no more."[11]

If our worldview does not allow for the Fire of God's Presence, we will not be inclined to seek it or draw near to it.

There are some deep truths and penetrating insights within the theological tradition of Churches of Christ, but in the important matter of intimacy with God and living in the Spirit it is deficient. Other American Protestant traditions, especially as they have become more settled in the mainstream and more accommodated to the modern spirit, share such deficiency.

The Barrier of Intellectualism

A second roadblock facing Churches of Christ is what we might call intellectualism. Those who stand behind this barrier, we could say, focus their energies primarily on analyzing the chemical properties of the Fire.

When we say that intellectualism is a barrier to participating in God's Life, we do not at all mean to disparage the intellect. But neither do we necessarily mean to praise it, for the human intellect or reasoning capacity is easily led astray and blinded by self-will. Human intellect or rationality is but a name for the processes by which we all attempt to perceive what is real and true and to maintain order in our conversations.

Rather, by intellectualism we are referring to what Soren Kierkegaard called the "theoretical attitude," the disengagement from God that turns God primarily into an object of critical investigation and debate, that hangs back from personal relationship with Him, that uses discussion about God as a means of avoiding God or perhaps thinks that in analyzing the things of God one is communing with Him.

Intellectualism is a subtle spiritual disease. Some of us stubbornly persist in the notion—no doubt because we happen to love intellectual things so much—that the fundamental solution is intellectual or academic. We cling to the notion that the hope of glory for the church lies mostly in the classroom or lecture hall. So things get reversed. Secondary things become primary things, and vice versa. Academic disciplines supersede Christian disciplines. One comes to spend far more time analyzing the chemical properties of Fire than in kneeling around the Fire and absorbing its warmth.

The modern academic environment bends some of us in that direction. We are trained to be critics, to be suspicious of "common" knowledge, to be wary of easy certainties. Our reflexes are trained to back off from things in order to view them coolly. We learn to distance ourselves from passionate commitments for fear of losing our "objectivity" or of believing too much. The fear of being unscholarly begins to loom larger than the fear of being unholy. Passion for God gets replaced by descriptions of passion for God.

This roadblock looms larger for some of us than others. Some of us easily let passion for theological and denominational issues displace passion for Jesus, prayer and life in the Spirit. Kierkegaard, observing this perpetual human tendency in nineteenth-century Denmark, said that if faced with two doors, one marked "Heaven" and the other "Lecture about Heaven," most would choose the lecture. Furthermore, critical analysis and polemics easily become consuming preoccupations. Too many people, Robert Richardson once wrote, "are ready to argue, debate, discuss, at all times, and will spend hours in the earnest defense of their favorite theories" but will not spend five minutes meditating "upon the character, the sayings, and perfections of Christ, or upon their own inward spiritual state."

The study of theology and related disciplines has a vital place in our relationship with God, just as the study of grammar has an important place in our learning to communicate with one another through language. Thus we have little patience with Billy Sunday's reported dismissal of theology: "I don't know any more about theology than a jackrabbit knows about ping-pong, but I'm on my way to glory." Theology's primary place is to discern and support what the Spirit is doing. It is the gyroscope on the ship of faith, not the engine. Theology helps balance and protect Spirit-quickened life, but it doesn't bring life. "The Spirit gives life" (2 Cor. 3:6).

Drawing upon Psalm 119, Martin Luther once said that a faithful theologian was made by three things: meditation, temptation and prayer. Meditation is the personal engagement with Scripture—not for sermons, not for lectures, but for meeting with God. Temptation is the desire to resist or rationalize what the Lord is speaking to us. And prayer is our reply to what the Lord is saying and our wrestling with the temptation to dispute and resist his word.[12] These things draw us toward the Fire.

Intellectualism does not just afflict academically-inclined Christians. It can become a way of life for any Christian. Kierkegaard's famous parable of "The Tame Geese" shows how.[13] A group of geese, he said, would go to church together every Sunday to worship. In his sermon the gander would always speak on the same theme: "the glorious destiny of geese, and the noble end for which their maker had created them." He would talk about how the creator had given them wings so they could fly away to distant pastures, and how that presently they were like strangers in a foreign land. Every time the creator's name was mentioned the lady-geese would curtsy and the ganders would bow their heads. And when the service was over the geese would waddle home.

None of the geese actually flew. They couldn't. They were so well fed by the farmer that they had long since grown too fat for flying. A few would attempt to take flying seriously. They would begin exercising their wings and trying to lose weight. But the others would express alarm or pity: "Well, now we certainly see where this leads, this wanting to fly. They lose weight. They don't thrive on God's grace like ourselves, for God's grace makes one plump, fat, and tasty." And Kierkegaard concludes: "The same is true of the worship of God in Christianity."

We can study aerodynamics for years but seldom get around to flying. We can get preoccupied with the chemistry of Fire but seldom find our spirits kindled by its warmth.

Suppression of the Affections

A third roadblock that keeps us from God's Life is suspicion of, and indeed suppression of, the affections. As we will see more fully in the next chapter, the modern world split reality apart, opening up gaping dualisms. One of these was a sharp split between reason and emotion. The realm of human feelings, affections or emotions was quickly demoted to a place of inconsequence, even scorn, in the exciting new venture of discovering, manipulating and harnessing the laws of nature through scientific rationality.

By the eighteenth century, nature, under the impact of the new science, had come to be viewed as a vast and precise machine. The cosmos, in short, was mechanized. Along with this new mechanistic view of nature came a new view of human nature. The essence of being human soon became the capacity for rational calculation and action. Reason and emotion, thinking and feeling, thus were placed in sharp opposition. As Stephen Toulmin put it, "Calculation was enthroned as the distinctive virtue of the human reason; and the life of the emotions was repudiated, as distracting one from the demands of clear-headed deliberation."[14] In modernity the emotions were messy, unstable things that interfered with the proper functioning of the mind.

The modern split between reason and emotion, to be sure, often provoked revolt. Romanticisms and revivalisms leaped to the other side of the chasm, exalting the emotions, decrying the intellect and thereby providing further evidence for modernity's case against emotion. Through it all, those on both sides of the chasm lost the profound wholeness of the human self that is captured in Scripture's focus on the "heart." This ancient metaphor points to the core of human selfhood, the very wellspring of beliefs, affections and attitudes. It is the wellspring for human actions, the deepest source of human transformation, the very center of our capacity for entering into friendship with God.

Diminishment of the affections diminishes our capacity to enter into the kind of personal relationship that God seeks with us. God seeks our friendship. Our trust. He desires us to find joy and pleasure in him. He invites our grief and lament. He woos us like a lover. He embraces us like a mother. He desires our love—heart, soul, mind and strength. Among the characteristics of the mature Christian life are those that are clearly affections: sorrow for sin, gratitude, compassion, joy, peace, love and hope.[15]

Scripture says: "Though you have not seen him, you love him; and even though you do not see him now, you believe in him and are filled with an inexpressible and glorious joy" (1 Pet. 1:8). Jonathan Edwards points out from this passage that true faith produces two dynamics in one's heart: love for Christ ("you love him") and joy in Christ ("glorious joy"). This happens because the new birth creates a new heart with a new will and new affections.

Without the engagement of the heart we do not really worship. The engagement of the heart means that our feelings, emotions and affections come alive. Jesus said of the Pharisees, "This people honors me with their lips, but their heart is far from me; in vain do they worship me" (Mt. 15:8-9). It is easy for us to worship with our lips and keep our hearts far from God. It is quite possible to say the prescribed words, to sing the songs, to go through the common motions, but to worship in vain. It is vain if it does not engage the heart. If we do not feel any grief for sin or longing or hope or fear or awe or gratitude or delight or need, then we can sing and pray and gesture as much as we like, but it will not be true worship.

There is of course an important distinction to be made between emotion and emotionalism. Emotion is the realm of the feelings and affections that make up our personhood and make relationships possible. Certain types of affections are called forth by Scripture's grand picture of God and His Kingdom, and appear to be considerably under human control. Indeed, in Scripture certain affective dispositions can be commanded: "Love your neighbor as yourself." "Rejoice with those who rejoice and weep with those who weep." "Rejoice in the Lord always." Being resentful or full of anger, Scripture seems to be saying, is not like being six feet tall or having male pattern baldness; rather, the feelings or affections can be ordered into new habits or dispositions through exercise of the will—dispositions in harmony with the new way of Jesus.

Emotionalism, on the other hand, is a dwelling in and seeking after certain kinds of emotion for their own sake. It leads worshippers to close in upon themselves, judging the worship experience solely by the measure of their own feelings, rather than moving beyond themselves into the grand and transforming realities of God's majesty and God's Kingdom.

Churches of Christ, more than many conservative Christians today, face the challenge of recovering a more holistic understanding of the affections and their central role in our life with

God. We have bought into the modern split so deeply and developed such strong doctrinal justifications for it that it will be difficult at this juncture to make healthy adjustments. Compounding the difficulty at present is the postmodern taste for all things affective, which will tend to further provoke the reactionary spirit that has long characterized Churches of Christ.

Despite these high and forbidding roadblocks, members of Churches of Christ today can—and some undoubtedly will—choose that more vibrant and fulsome Spiritual path pointed to, and to some extent marked out, by Robert Richardson. Though it has been long overgrown and mostly forgotten, that ancient (and indeed classic) path lies there ready to be rediscovered, cleared away and embarked upon again. The collapse of modernity and the crisis of decision that now confronts us makes recovery of that way both more possible and more attractive. In the next chapter we will sketch out some vital doctrinal features of that alternative way.

Notes

1. Diogenes Allen, *Christian Belief in a Postmodern World: The Full Wealth of Conviction* (Louisville, KY: Westminster/John Knox, 1989), 2-6. We are here adopting Allen's imagery but altering it for the sake of brevity and clarity.

2. Rene Descartes, *Meditations on First Philosophy*, trans. Laurence J. Lafleur (New York: Macmillan, 1951), 24. Descartes would not agree that this means we all think differently because he believed that reason was the same for all people. But his notion of autonomy eventually became what we are describing here.

3. Richard Middleton and Brian Walsh, *Truth is Stranger than it Used to Be: Biblical Faith in a Postmodern Age* (Downers Grove, IL: InterVarsity, 1995), 15-17.

4. Diogenes Allen, "Christian Values in a Post-Christian Context," in *Postmodern Theology: Christian Faith in a Pluralistic World*, ed. Frederick Burnham (San Francisco: Harper, 1989).

5. See the *Theological Dictionary of the New Testament*, ed. Gerhard Kittel.

6. Descartes, *Meditations*, 33.

7. Jaroslav Pelikan, *The Vindication of Tradition* (New Haven: Yale University, 1984).

8. In his moving Spiritual autobiography, *Beyond the Sacred Page*, Edward Fudge recounts a similar experience.

9. Charles H. Kraft, *Christianity with Power: Your Worldview and Your Experience of the Supernatural* (Ann Arbor, MI: Vine, 1989), 20.

10. Dallas Willard, *Hearing God: Developing a Conversational Relationship with God* (1984; new edition, Downers Grove, IL: InterVarsity, 1999), 107-108.

11. Karl Barth, *The Word of God and the Word of Man* (New York: Harper & Row, 1957).

12. Martin Luther, "Preface to the Wittenberg Edition of Luther's German Writings, 1539," in *Selected Writings of Martin Luther*, ed. Theodore G. Tappert (Philadelphia: Fortress , 1967), 1:9-11.

13. *The Diary of Soren Kierkegaard*, ed. Peter Rohde (New York: Philosophical Library, 1960), 177-79.

14. Stephen Toulmin, *Cosmopolis: The Hidden Agenda of Modernity* (New York: Free Press, 1990), 134.

15. For an excellent treatment of emotion and the formation of Christian character, see Robert C. Roberts, *Spirituality and Human Emotion* (Grand Rapids: Eerdmans, 1982), esp. 12-24.

5

The Heart of the Matter

In Chapter 4 we noted that modernity drove a wedge between us and God—and, as a result, between us and our own selves. This is the condition of estrangement that so marks the late modern and particularly the postmodern eras, and this is the immediate source of the crisis that faces us at the present crossroad. The world was split apart, and that split has run deeply through our own hearts. It has pierced our own selves, cleaving the realm of our reasoning from the realm of our feelings and affections, dividing the soul from the body, the physical from the spiritual. In this chapter we lay out more fully the nature of the split in the modern world, how it has effected us, and how central affirmations of the Christian faith enable healing of the split.

The World Split Apart

The word for a split apart world is dualism. Dualism has taken many forms in Christian history and always remains a constant threat. In its most basic form dualism claims that a great gulf separates God from humans and humans (spirit) from the natural world (matter). Many modern Western Christians are basically dualists (in their sub- or half-conscious world views). They believe that the physical world is essentially evil, that the "spiritual" world is good, and that God sent his Son to rescue us from this evil physical realm into a good spiritual realm. This leads them to uphold a split between the public and the private, the political and the religious, and to embrace a gospel that has little to do with space and time. Christianity has little to do with politics because its concerns are only for inward, "spiritual" and heavenly things.

The early Christian movement sought to reject dualism, especially of the "gnostic" sort. The lure of dualism was to deny or reject the good created order and seek to escape into a purely "spiritual" realm. Greek religion and classical theism moved powerfully and incessantly in this direction. The created, material realm was to be escaped, even despised; souls were meant to escape bodies, for bodies did nothing but inhibit the freedom and indeed the very being of the human spirit. So reality got carved up into two radically separate realms: the realm of matter and the realm of spirit. Matter was evil, nonmaterial spirit was good. The religious quest entailed coping with the material until achieving escape into the spiritual.

The main problem with such dualism is that it is not Christian. The Bible simply does not view human beings or creation this way. It does not distinguish between the physical, created world and the sphere of God's concern, involvement and activity.

In its modern, Enlightenment form, this old pagan and often-christianized dualism was continued with a vengeance, but the emphasis was reversed. The realm of matter was split sharply from the realm of spirit or timeless truths, as before, but now it was the realm of matter, not spirit, where one sought "salvation." For the old "gnostic" dualism the material world was an ashtray; for the new modern dualism the material world was a gold mine. For the new dualism God became a nuisance and got kicked upstairs, into the other realm, out of sight and out of the way, thus freeing human beings for mastery of the world of nature. Scientific rationality, as we have seen, became the new shrine; the brass heaven became the new canopy for the shrine.

Many modern Christians bought into this new dualism, just as many premodern Christians had bought into the early Greek dualism. To varying degrees they adopted the modern framework that sharply split off the natural realm from the supernatural. There was Nature with its fixed "laws"—newly discovered by Newton and company—and there was God's realm. God most surely created Nature's world and still took a passing interest in it. But Nature was a fixed and separate realm, operating by rigid (and wonderfully predictable) laws; indeed, God's intervention was not much needed. God inevitably became more and more of an absentee landlord who has left us pretty much to fend for ourselves as best we can. The split or the gulf between the two realms grew steadily wider as modernity progressed.

The mainstream of the Christian tradition bought into this split to one degree or another, for the pressure was enormous to fit their religion into the new mechanistic worldview. And it wasn't that difficult to do because, after all, one could still extol God as a powerful creator and view the world as a marvel of design and purpose. But the result of buying into the modern split, of course, was a diminished view of God's relationship with the creation. God became less personal, less active, less present. And many modern Christians found this new state of affairs quite congenial, for it allowed them to pursue their own (profitable) mastery of the new world without too much interference from God.

The acquiescence of modern Christians in this dualism spans the range from liberal to conservative. If liberals were too world-affirming, readily compromising the "supernatural" elements of the faith, conservatives were often too world-denying, readily compromising the creational elements of the faith. The "social gospel" was typically pitted against the "simple gospel," with some seizing upon the "social" as their gospel and others upon the "simple" as theirs. As N. T. Wright concluded, "a good deal of the Western church has not only acquiesced in dualism; it has often mistaken it for the gospel itself."[1]

As the new mechanistic worldview took shape in the seventeenth century, Christian thinkers began to draw a sharper line between the ordinary, natural course of the world, in which God was not directly involved, and the occasional (but rare) intervention by God. Some began to say that it would be beneath the dignity of God to intervene in nature for trivial reasons; indeed, some thought it would reflect on the quality of His original creative handiwork, for if God had made things right in the beginning, why would He need to intervene?

Christian thinkers in the seventeenth century established a new framework for thinking about God's location and about the nature of miracles (or divine intervention in the natural order). They increasingly split the natural off from the supernatural, making increasingly problematic the question of Divine Presence and action in the natural order. The world becomes a basically independent, machine-like realm in which God might sometimes intervene— though such intervention now becomes interruption or violation of the natural or normal course of things.

But the idea of a "natural" order independent of God, an order which God must "interrupt," is a modern idea that arose in the seventeenth century. In this view God is not active most of the time; sometimes (perhaps rarely or perhaps only in biblical times) God acts to interrupt the natural order. The modern view assumes that the world basically runs itself; the question is whether or to what extent God interferes. For example, God no longer causes the sun to rise (in fact, the sun does not rise); rather, planets rotate by themselves (somehow) and the sun is a fixed star. And so on.

The problem is that the Bible does not view things this way at all. The biblical writers assume that God is at work in all of this history. Some stories tell of dramatic divine activity, God's wonders: bushes burn unconsumed, seas get parted, lepers get healed, apostles get freed from prison. In many other biblical stories no such wonders occur. But God is seen as just as much at work. The biblical writers seem little concerned to distinguish or reflect on these different modes of God's activity. For them God is everywhere at work in the world, occasionally in notably dramatic ways and often through the more usual means of circumstance and human action.[2]

So when we glibly pronounce that God can work in the world and in our lives but only in a "non-miraculous" way we speak in categories created in the seventeenth century, not in biblical categories. Such a way of speaking, in fact, became possible only in the split apart world of the Enlightenment. Specifically, the Bible recognizes no dualism between nature and super nature, the world of scientific laws and the world of Divine intervention. Therefore, it makes no sense biblically to define a miracle as "God's suspending the rules of nature"—there were no such rules. Instead, life is imbued by God's activity, sometimes in dramatic, extraordinary ways, other times in more mundane but no less "miraculous" ways.[3]

Modernity was a world split apart: mind versus body (Descartes); reason versus faith; fact versus feeling; visible versus invisible; sacred versus secular; public versus private. These splits or dualisms, as they have widened throughout the modern period, have left us lonely and estranged, confused and isolated. The new spiritual openness and searching of our time is a response to this situation.

The Christian faith, properly understood, has the resources to heal this split-apart world. As we will see throughout the remainder of this book, our central resource is the doctrine of the Trinity. It provides our anchor against all dualisms. For many—perhaps most—modern Christians this claim may sound strange. For to them the doctrine of the Trinity itself is a huge problem. But we want to show how the Trinity, rather than being itself a problem, is rather the answer to a problem. That problem is the problem of dualism. Charles Cochrane, in his classic work *Christianity and Classical Culture*, shows how in the age of Augustine the Trinity made possible the healing of the dualisms—between the sensible and the intelligible, the eternal and the temporal, the personal and the impersonal—that pagan religion and classical thought could not resolve. The same is true for the dualisms of modernity. That is why we are presently seeing a wonderfully creative renewal of Trinitarian doctrine.

The Triumph of God

A world split between nature and super nature (or spirit) and human nature split between body and soul is not the way God intended it. In fact, such fragmentation is precisely what is being overcome through the work of God in Christ and in His Spirit. In the words of Paul, God is leading us "in a triumphal procession" through history as His Word and, indeed, even His Life is spread to every corner of the world (2 Cor. 2: 14-17).

To understand how God's present triumph in history is overcoming the countless splits and fragmentations we have imposed upon this life, we must first understand the way the biblical story unfolds. Often we read the Bible in a uniform way, reading Leviticus as if it had the same function and nearly the same message as Daniel or John. The other, opposite temptation is to read the Bible as if the Hebrew Scripture, the "Old Testament," does not matter or, at least, does not matter as much as the New. To our modern way of thinking these two parts of God's Word must be pitted against one another, one must take priority over the other, one must fade and the other must become dominant.

This way of viewing the Bible is simply unfair to the way God reveals Himself in Scripture. We do not see a God in the Bible who reveals Himself and then turns to efface that revelation with another, "better" revelation. Instead, God reveals Himself through and in the midst of a plan. There is a grand narrative to Scripture, a deep and involved plan of which God Himself is a part. Within this plan there is movement: there is movement away from God and movement toward God. He is the one who makes the plan, but in a strange way He is also part of the plan. He makes the plan, but the shift in movement is only possible when He enters the plan (the Incarnation), and then re-enters it at every instant (the Holy Spirit). We will focus in the next few pages on that plan, and then indicate the way in which God is part of His plan as well.

Recall for a moment the dualisms of the last section. What caused them? The long answer involves an in-depth discussion of modern philosophy and reaches further back into Greek philosophy.

But, to press further, what is the source of the dualisms in modern and Greek philosophies? Why are humans constantly tempted to split the world into clean and opposing pairs (or worse)? What accounts for our incessant desire to fragment this world, to divide it into innumerable pieces and then to raise one piece up against the others?

The answer lies several thousand years in humanity's past, but it is a past that is far from "done with" in the present. Genesis tells us the story of the Tower of Babel. At that time humanity spoke with one tongue, reasoned with one mind. In one universal language these ancient people laid out their plans to erect an enormous tower in the middle of the earth's central city. In the words of Genesis, humanity did this to "make a name for themselves." God saw this and was unhappy. He disrupted their plans and scattered the languages of humankind so that humanity would never be able to scale the heights of Divinity again.

Why God scattered their language and disrupted their plans is unclear. Traditionally, the answer has been that the human unity was forged in pride, the kind of pride that would entice them to build a tower to heaven. This answer may be somewhat facile, but it at least captures one side of what was happening. Humans were indeed erecting an edifice to themselves, and indeed, this edifice threatened to assume the role of God. As a result, God scattered their languages.

The result of such a scattering is the fragmentation of God's image in the human heart and on the earth as a whole. Man and woman had already become disjointed in the Garden, brothers became estranged with Cain's murder, now human communities are also revealed as disconnected and prone to idolatry. The community that gathered at Babel desired to establish a towering reminder of its greatness for all generations, but such a desire reveals that communities will always have a penchant for putting their own interest before God's. Idolatry, more simply, is the sin of the state more than it is the sin of the individual.

Yet a more fundamental point should not be lost here: the relationships between men and woman, between people and nature, and between people within one community are disrupted because the most fundamental relationship of all has been disrupted. When our relationship with God is askew, every relationship in life reflects that primary distortion. The story of the Tower of Babel demonstrates this brokenness by the simple fact that the diversity of languages leads to a broken unity among humanity.

In the Old Testament God works within the strict confines of broken relationships. He heals, leads, triumphs, forgives and speaks in the context of broken relationships. Through His prophets He also speaks of a time when those relationships will be mended, when there will be fellowship across global, political, ethnic and gender lines (see for example Joel 2, Jeremiah 31, and Isaiah 11). The Old Testament tells a story of broken relationships and amazing, irreducible acts of grace within those broken relationships. We cannot understand the significance of Jesus, much less of the Holy Spirit, unless we understand the tragedy of brokenness (that is, broken relationships) into which they enter on behalf of God.

Galatians 3:28 seems to be a very simple, familiar and unsurprising verse until one reads it against the backdrop of the tragedy: "There is no longer Jew or Greek, there is no longer slave or free, there is no longer male or female; for all of you are one in Christ Jesus." This verse tells us that history is moving in another direction, that we are moving out of brokenness and into unity. But this is far from the only Scriptural indicator that history is moving in another direction. Consider the scandalous inclusion of woman, the reaching out to the "unclean," the incessant crossing of religious and political lines in the ministry of Jesus. Consider God's revelation to Peter that the Gentiles are to be included in the Kingdom of God. Consider Paul's life ministry to the Gentiles, his passion for unity revealed in 1 Corinthians, and his refusal to elevate anyone, even an apostle, above any other Christian in God's Kingdom. Consider all of this against the backdrop of the tragedy of Babel, the confusion of languages, the fragmentation of the world, and the resultant acts of violence and oppression seen in the history of Israel. Something has changed; the momentum of history has shifted in a radical way.

One episode in particular emphasizes a shift in direction or a new momentum in God's plan. From the story of the Tower of Babel we learn that when humans, acting out of pride, seek to unify themselves, they are scattered and their languages are confused. With this in mind, jump ahead several thousand years to Pentecost. Here we see the coming together of many nationalities to hear God's Word preached by Peter. But the results of Babel make this impossible— how can these diverse people understand the unifying message of Peter? Quite simply, God intervenes and allows the Apostles to speak in languages that everyone present can understand.

The structure is the exact opposite of Babel's: at Babel a unified humanity comes together to celebrate its own unity and is scattered by God; at Pentecost fragmented humanity comes together to hear from God and God makes that word available to everyone in their own language. The result is that unity, though not achieved, is given. The sign of this new unity is that many diverse people are baptized into the one, unified name of Christ Jesus. Babel is reversed and continues to be reversed each time God remakes very different people into brothers and sisters.

The Bible presents a grand ebb and flow in the history of humanity. As humanity digresses further from God's Presence they become disjointed, fragmented and violent. But with the coming of Christ, humanity begins to move in the opposite direction: toward unity, toward wholeness and toward peace. The ministry of Jesus, the expansion of the church, and Paul's intolerance for disunity should be read in the light of this grand march, this triumphal procession that leads into the heart of our One God.

This is a grand and large vision. It is one that is very fittingly, though ironically, called apocalyptic. Put simply, our apocalyptic vision tells us that the secret to human history, the reason the world has not yet come to an end, is that God is presently working to bring together a new people. This new people is not another race separate from others through racial, geographical or gendered borders. Instead it is one composed of every nation, speaking every tongue, characterized by peace, and shaped by the slain lamb whom they recognize as the Lion of Judah (Rev. 5).[4] This is our secret vision; this is the way we understand history. This is how we interpret our relative gains and losses.

We should not forget, however, that the triumph of God through the triumphal procession of His people is a procession very much in progress. The triumph of God is not fulfilled yet, not everywhere at least. More importantly, neither should we forget that the triumph of God comes from God and not from us. Every time we seek to unify ourselves through our own power we reap the same tragedy displayed at Babel. Humans can only forge unities apart from God by excluding other elements of creation or other people inscribed by God's image. This is exactly how we should view the Greek and Modern dualisms we described in the previous section.[5]

The Greek attempt to establish unity upon the invisible soul led many to abuse their bodies, to threaten the physical lives of non-believers with the sword in order to "save their souls,'" and to disparage the goodness of God's creation. The modern attempt to glorify nature at the expense of the Spiritual has led to the depreciation of faith, the violent reduction of reality to the factual, and the separation of morality from technique—a separation which has given us the A-bomb among countless other immoral weapons of mass destruction. These are but the outward manifestations of more deeply felt consequences, as we shall see in the following chapter.

God is leading His people into the unity of His Son, but the world will always rebel by trying to find a more "certain" unity in something that humans possess. Thus in the present age God is unifying His people by bringing them together in a manner that honors their diversity. But the world—the realm where the forces of disunity, of violent fragmentation, of dualisms rage—continues to counter His purposes. We know the end though. We know that God will be triumphant come what may. In the meantime, we taste God's unity. To understand how, we must turn to the central way in which God brings the unity and wholeness to us that He reveals in the Life of Jesus. The Spirit of God restores our lost wholeness by bringing us into the Presence of the source of holiness.

Real Presence

God's unity comes to us through the work of God Who Is Spirit, yet the pervasive misunderstandings of the Spirit often diminish our experience of God's triumph. Churches of Christ have minimized the role of the Spirit, while other traditions have often talked of the Spirit aimlessly, as if the Spirit can be easily equated with most any feeling or experience. Contrary to both impulses, the Spirit assumes a large and clear role in the narrative of Scripture. There is a clear direction in Scripture, a clear direction in which God moves closer to us—indeed, into us. God is restoring the creational unity and wholeness we have lost. It is a grand and marvelous plan. In this section we paint a broad picture of the Spirit's work in that movement.

The Bible often uses the imagery of fire to speak of God's Presence. Moses encountered the Lord in the desert in the form of a burning bush (Ex. 3:2; Acts 7:30). The Israelites were guided by a cloud by day and a pillar of fire so they could travel by night (Ex. 13:21-22;Ps. 78:14), and when they set up the tabernacle the cloud rested over it "like the appearance of fire until morning" (Num. 9:15). Moses on one occasion said to the Lord, "You are in the midst of this people; for you, O Lord, art seen face to face; and your cloud stands over them and you go before them, in a pillar of cloud by day and in a pillar of fire by night" (Num. 14:14).

When Moses brought the Israelites to the foot of Mt. Sinai to meet God, the Lord appeared on the mountain "in fire" and the whole mountain shook (Ex. 19:18). Moses went up on the mountain and the "glory of the Lord" settled upon it: "Now the appearance of the glory of the Lord was like a devouring fire on the top of the mountain in the sight of the people of Israel" (Ex. 24:17). And the Lord spoke to the people "out of the midst of the fire," with Moses standing between the people and the Lord (Deut. 5:4-5; 9:10).

In Israel's early worship fire symbolized God's continual Presence. To the priests who conducted worship at the tabernacle the Lord said: "Fire shall be kept burning upon the altar continually; it shall not go out" (Lev. 6:12-13).

When John preached about the coming Christ, he said, "He will baptize you with the Holy Spirit and with fire" (Lk. 3:16). On Pentecost the descent of the Holy Spirit is accompanied by "tongues of fire" (Acts 2:3). "Do not put out the Spirit's fire," Paul admonished the Thessalonians (5:19). In Scripture fire generally represents God's action upon the earth, whether it be in revealing His glory, in purifying the sinner or in bringing the divine judgment. "Our God is a consuming fire" (Heb. 12:29).

The symbol of fire is one important way that Scripture portrays a central fact about God: He makes himself present among His people. God has come into their midst and dwells with them. The experience of God's Presence thus became central in the life of Israel's worship.

The book of Exodus provides key insight into the theme of God's Presence. After the Lord delivers Israel from bondage in Egypt, Moses leads the people through the desert to Mt. Sinai, the place where God "dwells." As we have seen, the Lord appeared in fire, and Moses goes up the mountain into the Lord's Presence. After the Lord gives the Ten Commandments (Ex. 20-24), He gives Moses precise instructions for building a tabernacle (25-31). This tabernacle marks a change in the way God is present to His people.

God plans to "move" from the mountain and dwell among His covenant people by means of this tent. His Presence will no longer be associated with the top of a mountain; God will come down to dwell with them (Ex.25:8; 29:42-3). No longer will they need, as Moses did, to ascend to God on the mountain.

But when Moses comes down from the mountain where he has received these instructions, he finds the people worshipping a golden calf they have made. They have broken their promise to Yahweh and spurned their new relationship with Him, so the Lord instructs them to depart for the land of promise but announces to Moses that "my presence will not go with you." An angel will go instead. But Moses pleads with the Lord: "if your Presence does not go with us, do not send us up from here. How will anyone know that you are pleased with me and with your people unless you go with us? What else will distinguish me and your people from all the other people on the face of the earth?" (33:15-16). The Lord grants Moses' request, then reveals His glory to Moses in a new way.

The actual construction of the tabernacle follows (Ex. 35-39). When it was finished the cloud came to rest upon it and "the glory of the Lord filled the tabernacle" (40:35). The tabernacle became not just a symbol of God's Presence but a space filled up with God, a place of Real Presence. God's presence was not confined to the tabernacle but there was an intensity or glory of Presence not true of any other place.

With the sanctuary of Presence in their midst, Israel set off for the land of promise and the place in it which "the Lord your God will choose as a dwelling for his name" (Deut. 12:11). That new dwelling, completed only many years later, was Solomon's temple. When it was completed "the glory of the Lord descended and filled the temple" (1 Kgs. 8:11). The Lord's Presence dwelt there.

But Israel's tragic failures led eventually to the departure of the Lord's Presence. In exile Ezekiel saw a vision of the departure of God's glory from the Jerusalem temple (Ezek. 11:22-23). The exiles in Babylon became a people no longer marked by the Presence of the living God in their midst. But Ezekiel envisioned a time of God's dramatic return: "As the glory of the Lord entered the temple by the gate facing east, the Spirit lifted me up and brought me into the inner court; and behold, the glory of the Lord filled the temple" (Ezek. 43:5).

In his visions Ezekiel also saw a valley of dry bones: they were the bones of Israel, exiled and barren of the Presence. And Israel says: "Our bones are dried up, and our hope is lost; we are clean cut off" (37:11). But the Lord says: "A new heart I will give you and a new spirit I will put within you; and I will take out of your flesh the heart of stone and give you a heart of flesh....And I will put my Spirit within you, and you shall live" (Ezek. 36:26-7; 37:14).

In the New Testament Paul the Apostle picks up these very themes to make a striking point: in the new covenant, the Holy Spirit fulfills these promises. Paul draws explicitly upon the Old

Testament imagery of God dwelling among His people by means of tabernacle and temple. Now, Paul says, the living God indwells His temple once again: the church is being built into a" holy temple" as "a dwelling place for God by his Spirit" (Eph. 2:22). And not only has God again taken up residence in the midst of His people, but He has also taken up residence in the lives of individual Christians: "Do you not know that you are God's temple, and that God's Spirit really dwells in you?" (1 Cor. 3:16; also 2 Cor. 6:16).

The Spirit is God's personal Presence among His people. The Spirit is now the way God dwells in His holy temple, and we, the church, are that temple. As God's Presence "filled" Moses' tabernacle and Solomon's temple, so we can be "filled" with the Spirit or the "fullness" of God (Eph. 5:18; 3:19). Christians are people who affirm and experience God's Real Presence.

In addition to the temple imagery, Paul also draws from Ezekiel and Jeremiah to show that the Spirit is the way God has fulfilled the new covenant. He says that the Corinthians have received the new covenant, thus they are God's letter, written by "the Spirit of the living God, not on tablets of stone but on tablets of human hearts" (2 Cor. 3:3). Paul says that they are ministers of this new covenant and that it was delivered "in the Spirit," not in a written code. As with Ezekiel (37:14), Paul underscores that "the Spirit gives life" (3:6). Christ through his death and resurrection effected the new covenant, but the Spirit makes that covenant a powerful reality among the covenant community, the church.

The Lord had promised, "I will dwell among them [again] and they shall be my people" (Ezek 37:27). For Paul this promise was fulfilled through the Holy Spirit. The Spirit is none other than the way God's Presence has returned to His people. Thus, when a pagan comes into the Christian assembly and his heart is laid open as the Spirit moves in the prophetic gift, Paul says, he will "worship God and declare that God is really among you" (1 Cor. 14:24-25).

Pentecost was the grand event that stands as a milepost of the age of fulfillment. As N. T. Wright summarizes:

The early Christians, soon after Jesus' ascension, began to experience God in a way previously only known in very limited circles, particularly among prophets and other great leaders of God's people. They experienced God living within them, coming upon them like a new wind given to be their own breath, like a fire that burned without consuming them. And this new life was stamped with a recognizable character. It was the life of Jesus himself. The risen Christ had gone from their sight; but, as he had promised, a wind from God came and took possession of them, and they knew that this wind or breath or Spirit, was the living presence of the living God, the God they had come to see most clearly in Jesus (John 14:16-17).[6]

God is really among his people as God Who Is Spirit. We experience Him. He moves and works in our lives. He quickens and comforts, transforms and tests. He empowers our prayers and arms us in our struggle against the "powers."

We live in the "dispensation of the Spirit" and so can behold greater splendor than Moses did. We can move into his Presence and behold his glory in a way that Moses could not. Moses veiled his face when he came down the mountain from the Lord's Presence. The temple also had a veil shielding people from God's Presence. But the Spirit of the Lord has removed the veil. We can enter the holy place and stand in the very Presence of God. With unveiled faces we can behold the glory of the Lord and in that Presence be changed from one degree of glory to another (2 Cor. 3:12-18).

In the Christian worship assembly we affirm this Presence in a particular and focused way. We claim the Scriptural promise that when we come together in the name of Christ, the Risen One is present with us (Mt. 18:20). As James McClendon carefully words it, "This holy presence cannot be reduced to our awareness or 'experience' of the presence....The promise is not, 'Where two or three are gathered, you will have such and such worship experiences.' He only promised to be at hand." Jesus' real presence in worship is not a function of our feelings or experiences or eyesight. We affirm His presence by faith, claiming the Scriptural promise. "If we do not sense his presence," McClendon continues, "there he is yet, hidden, perhaps ignored or forgotten, perhaps officially banished from our worship by someone's theology. Yet there. Nor is his presence merely a hyperbolic expression for the presence of other believers: we are there, and he is." Certainly the church is called "Christ's body" (1 Cor. 12:27); but Christ's presence in the assembly is more than that. More also than the ordinances or signs—baptism, preaching and the Lord's Supper. Christ is "present in his own right, as one of the fellowship, as a witness to our baptisms, as a listener to the preached word, as a sharer at the holy table." As well-schooled moderns, we reflexively want to ask: "If Christ is really present, then why don't I see Him?" And the answer is that "he elects now to be present thus and not otherwise."[7] In the Christian assembly we meet with Christ, and there, through the Spirit of Christ, partake of the Divine Life.

This talk of "real presence" may well seem strange—maybe even fantastic—to many of us. The degree that it does is probably a good measure of the distance we moderns have come from the world of Scripture—and a measure of the distance we must travel to re-enter that world.

Conclusion

As Christians we enter into a relationship with God that runs deeper than the most profound human relationships. As a result we can experience moments of the deepest joy imaginable, witness the immeasurable depths of God's power, feel some of the unutterable sadness of human sin, and experience moments of sheer ecstasy in worship. In short, we participate in the Life of our God.

But here is the crucial point: these various experiences through which we participate in God's Life are not aimless experiences. The personal benefits we receive from experiencing God's deep involvement in our lives are certainly noteworthy. Indeed, we should celebrate them with other Christians. We should not be embarrassed to name the moments of joy, healing, sadness, elation and sheer ecstasy that God gives us. But simply recognizing and naming these moments is not enough. And simply seeking after them for selfish reasons is utterly inappropriate. As Christians we are called to a far larger task: to locate the significance of these experiences within the larger context of God's Triumphal Procession.

We spoke earlier of the tendencies of some church traditions to diminish the role of God's Spirit and, at the other extreme, of the excessive and aimless "spiritualisms" found in other church traditions. Both tendencies stop short of God's grand vision. Our experiences of God's Life must be brought into the light, not for their own sake, but so we can see and participate in God's work of restoring the unity of creation. The fire of God's Presence continues to burn brightly that we may experience the grand unity He is bringing, that we may be prompted into acts reflecting that unity, that we may see more clearly the present unfolding of the biblical drama, and that we may catch glimpses of the glorious end of all things. When a prayer is answered, for example, we should see in this singular act the work of God in overcoming the seemingly hopeless fragmentation and brokenness of human life.

The following chapters develop two key doctrines that safeguard this rich and dynamic relationship with God. In the dulling routines of everyday life the fire of God's Presence easily becomes a flicker. Sin patterns and unbelief often make God's Triumphal Procession seem like little more than a dream. And worship caught in the clutches of traditionalism makes the Temple seem empty. We lose the sense of participating in God's Life. And as that sense recedes, the old dualisms return (between worship and "real life" for example), further impeding our vision of the Procession, perhaps even impeding the Procession itself.

Thus the questions we address in the next section are: How can we (a) maintain our vision of God's Triumphal Procession, (b) focus our experiences with God toward that Procession, and (c) keep at bay the dualisms that tempt us? In answering these questions we will develop two most vital Christian ideas: the view of the human self as relational, and the corresponding view of God's Life as Trinitarian or relational. These ideas can in no way substitute for the fire of God's Presence; but they can, at least, fuel the flames of God's Presence in our own awareness and keep us from common abuses, denials and excesses. We thus turn next to a biblical understanding of God's participation in our lives.

Notes

1. N. T. Wright, *Bringing the Church to the World: Renewing the Church to Confront the Paganism Entrenched in Western Culture* (Minneapolis, MN: Bethany House, 1992), 21.

2. John Calvin in the sixteenth century sought to uphold this biblical sense of "miracle": "For there are as many miracles of divine power as there are kinds of things in the universe, indeed, as there are things either great or small." *Institutes of the Christian Religion* 1.14.21 He refused to distinguish one class of events as uniquely miraculous; occasionally events occur that seem to violate radically the normal order but they serve only to remind us that God is directing the course of normal events as well.

3. See William Placher, *The Domestication of Transcendence: How Modern Thinking about God Went Wrong* (Louisville, KY: Westminster/John Knox, 1996), 128-45.

4. See James McClendon, Jr., *Systematic Theology: Doctrine* (Nashville: Abingdon, 1994), 98-99.

5. This is one of the key biblical insights of the Christian philosopher Herman Dooyeweerd (along with many others in the Calvinist tradition). See, for example, Herman Dooyeweerd, *Roots of Western Culture: Pagan, Secular, and Christian Options* (Wedge, 1979), 7-39.

6. Wright, *Bringing the Church to the World*, 202-3.

7. McClendon, *Doctrine*, 379.

Part III

An Alternate Road

The living God longs for us to participate in the Divine Life, to know Him personally and enjoy Him. The doctrine of the Trinity is the essential doctrinal framework guiding and protecting such experience. And for a tradition without language to speak of encountering, experiencing and enjoying God, it provides the language.

6

Recovering Relationality: Toward a Trinitarian Spirituality

In the previous chapters we have examined the way that the modern worldview splits reality into pieces, diminishes the fundamental way we relate to God, and holds a view of human nature that imposes unfair and unbiblical demands upon us. Philosophers like Descartes would have us live as self-ruled, merely rational agents and ignore basic dimensions of human experience (such as faith and the affections). Locke would have us believe that our minds' are mere machine-like factories producing ideas that mirror nature and ignore the work of God's Spirit in our minds and hearts. These modern notions and impulses became part of the Stone-Campbell tradition at an early stage and remain strongly with us today.

Thus far we have pointed to the deficiencies of this modern mindset, showing that it is actually counter-productive to a fuller restoration of New Testament Christianity. Richardson gives us the barest outlines of an alternative path by attempting to recover a functional doctrine of the Spirit and to expel the modern tendencies of many Restorationists. Richardson's challenge, his vision and the controversy it created represent the crossroad of 1857.

We have also claimed that we are standing at a new crossroad, one not altogether different from the 1857 crossroad. We have described that crossroad in part by showing how the crisis of modernity stems from the collapse of modernity's brass heaven (chapters 4 and 5). The thought of Descartes, Locke and their modern colleagues is now widely judged too narrow for the dynamic, unpredictable and meaning-laden conditions of this life. In this chapter we want to travel further down Richardson' path, pointing to a doctrine—the Trinity—that can help us avoid the deep and alluring pitfalls along the more dominant, modern path. But most importantly, we want to show how the doctrine of the Trinity recovers something very biblical and very positive about God's nature and work.

If the title of this chapter strikes you as unusual and even a bit arid you are not alone. The word "Trinitarian" may be particularly vexing. It has been avoided by many in our tradition—and with some justification. To speak of the Trinity, it has been argued, is to speak of heavenly mysteries, bad mathematics, irrational philosophy and, more to the point, to speak of God in nonbiblical terms. Maybe the word simply stirs a vague sense of arcane and tedious theological riddles where the logic of round pegs fitting square holes is supposed to make sense.

So let us begin with a disclaimer: we find such discussions every bit as boring and irrelevant as you probably do. Our focus here is not to make the Trinity "make sense" and we have little at stake in the actual term "Trinity." Understanding how God is Three and at the same time One according to the rules of logic is as irrelevant as it is boring. The word "Trinity" itself is as good as any other word for describing what we are getting at and so we have opted to keep it. We want to be candid about exactly what we think of the word: it is not a revealed word, but the history and dynamics of Divine relationships that it describes is indeed revealed in Scripture. As one major theologian put it, Trinitarian doctrine "simply states explicitly what is implicit already in God's revelation in Jesus Christ."[1] We therefore use the word as a helpful way to summarize the basic biblical revelation of God's nature and as a useful tool for expelling some very unbiblical concepts. For many, such concepts have distorted the biblical understanding of God and such distortions have further stunted their Spiritual growth.

In this chapter we seek to sketch a picture of God, a picture that will allow this rich doctrine to seize the heart, excite the imagination and possibly confound the understanding as it has for many Christians through the centuries. The Bible reveals a God whose being is too fecund to be circumscribed in words, too mysterious to be contained within our understandings, and too personally involved with us to be reduced to a concept.

In Chapter 4 we introduced a "new" conception of the self—a relational self. Our claim was that to recover the full sense of the Divine Presence we need to begin thinking differently about human identity. We showed how ideas such as rational autonomy have functioned as road blocks to Divine-human interaction in the present. Now we need to reopen that conversation. To experience what Peter describes as "participation in the Divine nature" (2 Pet. 1:4) we need to begin with the most fundamental questions about both human nature and the Divine nature. In other words, we need to begin at the beginning: who is God and who are we according to the Bible? Peter gives us the first clue: whatever we are and whoever God is, we are able to participate in the very "nature" of God.

Before turning to these seemingly new, though very old, understandings of the self and of God, we first must re-examine modern autonomy. The doctrine of the Trinity becomes more inviting as we see it against the backdrop of such modern notions. Because autonomy has influenced us so deeply, the ideas in this chapter may seem somewhat foreign. In fact, many of us perhaps never realized there was an alternative to the modern view. There is an alternative, and we believe that pursuing it is the best and most sound way for Christians to flourish in the midst of our postmodern crisis.

This rival understanding of the self and God is best understood with the word relational. In the modern era—the era of Descartes, Locke, Campbell and Fanning—relationships were viewed as diminishing.

Human nature was not defined by its dependency on God but by its own reasoning abilities. Relationships stood in the way of autonomy. In the course of our discussion we want to claim the exact opposite: relationships are so integral to our nature that we cannot even understand who we are if we do not first understand how God relates to us. But because human autonomy has become so pervasive in our thinking, we begin our discussion with the human self and not with God. We will work backwards so to speak: we will begin with the question of the self in order to find its answer in God.

The Autonomous Self

If one asks, "What does it mean to be human?" Descartes, Locke and many other modern thinkers would reply, "The answer lies within you and you alone." Though they did not intend this to mean that the answer is different for every individual, we do hear echoes of this inward turn in the individualism of Western culture. We are inundated by commercials, pop songs, billboards and political speeches with this message. "The nobility of the individual," "the inalienable rights of the individual," "the freedom to make of myself whatever I chose"—these are the daily echoes of Descartes in our time. All these slogans and messages have one thing in common: they insist that nothing and no one has the right to tell us who we are. We are responsible for coming up with who we are individually.

God's Word about Autonomy

What if they are wrong? What if human autonomy—the idea that I alone rule myself—is simply a bad or false idea? What if the desire for self-rule is not a lofty truth about our nature to be celebrated but a sinful urge to be resisted?

The story of Adam's fall teaches us that self-rule is partially possible but in no way desirable (Gen. 2-3). We learn that Jesus, acting as our example, "emptied himself" of any lofty position to which he was entitled out of obedience to the Father and love for us (Phil. 2:6-7). Jesus further demonstrates the very character of God by washing his disciples feet, telling us through his actions that fulfillment comes in serving others, not in ruling ourselves (John 13:1-20). In Galatians 5 Paul emphasizes the priority of service, the law of love and the willingness to give up even the freedom we have in Christ (Gal. 5: 13-15). The Bible goes to great lengths to emphasize the importance of continually giving up pretensions to autonomy out of love for one another and in obedience to God.

In the following pages we will describe the idea of autonomy as it originated in modern thought. Many of these modern thinkers were devout men of faith who lived honorable lives (Descartes, Locke and Immanuel Kant were all Christians.) This should not lead us to conclude that their ideas were Christian (as Fanning conclud-ed about Locke) or, conversely, that because their ideas were not Christian they were evil (as those of us who disagree with them are tempted to do). We should conclude rather that they failed to see a gaping discrepancy between their ideas and some of the most fun-damental principles of their Christian faith. In their formulation and celebration of autonomy they were mistaken.

But their mistake has had tragic consequences, and we should not soft-pedal these out of respect for their lives. Autonomy began as a bad idea and has now become the sophisticated expression of some of our most selfish and sinful desires. The Bible teaches us that we were not created to rule ourselves, that we cannot fully rule over ourselves alone, that the attempt to rule over ourselves alone is rebellion against God's rule over us, and, finally, that when we try to rule over ourselves alone we reap only despair, loneliness and futility. As we examine the modern development of this apostate notion we should not be deceived by the rhetoric of our culture. The nobility of the individual does not rest in self-rule but in the fact that human nature is created in God's image (Gen. 1:26-27) and grows into an imperfect reflection of that same image (2 Cor. 3:18).

Modern philosophers failed to see these essential teachings of the Bible. Descartes claimed, as we have previously seen, that we are by nature "thinking things." He believed that the most basic clue to human nature, that which makes an individual uniquely human and noble, is the fact that he can, without any outside influence, think rational thoughts. When we speak of autonomy we are referring to this Cartesian idea—that being human and being an individual, rational agent are the same thing. More precisely, any "thing" capable of rational thought is human, any "thing" incapable (or thought incapable by the majority) is less than human.

It is significant that Descartes and his heirs used the word "man" and not human. They did not intend the term to include both males and females. Like most thought leaders in that era, they did not believe women, people of different races, children and anyone outside of their "civilized" world were fully rational. Neither then were they fully human. This assumption, in turn, was used to justify centuries of psychological and physical violence toward such groups. The mistreatment of minorities and women should indicate to us that the idea of autonomy, according to its own presuppositions, is exclusivist. Certainly we have expanded their circle of autonomy in our day, but rational autonomy will always exclude certain groups from its privileged circle of protection. Aside from the continuation of racism and patriarchy, one only has to look at the abortion rate to see how those thought incapable of rational thought are treated in American society.

It is no exaggeration to say that autonomy or individual self-rule was the most cherished concept in modernity. And it remains, arguably, the most cherished assumption in the Western world. Those who have bought into the myth of autonomy have failed, and continue to fail, to see the practical effects it has on human relationships.

The Rise of Autonomy, the Fall of Relationships
As the Cartesian idea of autonomy became more influential and more pronounced, the positive role of human relationships has receded. From the beginning of the modern age relationships were suspect. These early moderns were reacting against the totalitarian social institutions and traditions of their day, which all too often included the church. These institutions often sought to control and coerce human beings, and so we can easily understand Descartes' desire to distance himself from such institutions and

traditions. But it is the place to which he ran in reaction that has caused the problem.

These modern thinkers became so deeply suspicious of inherited traditions and the institutions that maintained them that they attempted a clean break from them. They turned solely to their own reasoning abilities. They reduced all truth, meaning and purpose to what they, themselves, could discover through reason. Their rejection of authoritarian traditions became a rejection of all traditions—and then a rejection of anything beyond the reaches of their own individual reason.

This stance affected their view of relationships at a very practical level. Because they felt manipulated, deceived and misled by their traditions, they vowed to trust no one for their beliefs unless they themselves could test such beliefs rationally. Their disparaging view of human relationships arose out of a breakdown of the one essential attribute of all relationships: trust. This exchange of trust for rational certainty is the foundation of modern autonomy.

It is not surprising that Descartes' method for finding reliable knowledge began as a vow to trust nothing. He began, that is, by doubting everything, including God's existence. In the modern world the path to certainty involves doubt, refusing to trust what is given, even one's own thought processes. This unwillingness to trust any outside authority created the impression that humans form trusting relationships only at great risks to themselves. In time the emphasis on human self-rule, along with the rejection of all outside influences on this rule, led to damaging and anti-biblical assumptions about human identity.

Relationships quickly came to be seen as quasi-contractual arrangements between two self-governed people. They were not to be forged upon trust but upon reason: one party possesses something the other needs and vice versa. Thus human relationships increasingly were viewed through the grid of utility—as a mutually beneficial exchange between two independent, isolated parties.

Through a long and convoluted history, a modified version of Descartes' notion of individual autonomy became deeply ingrained in late-modern culture. One only has to look at the divorce rates, and then deeper at the reasons cited for divorce, to see that most view themselves as self-ruled. When the relationship ceases to be a mutually beneficial exchange between independent parties, when the demands of a spouse require a deep enough sacrifice of autonomy, the relationship is often aborted. Or one need only observe the contemporary obsession with individual "rights" to detect the echo of Descartes. The self-evident rights guaranteed by our constitution (which is very much at home with the modern version of the self) has grown to outlandish and impossible proportions.

In the modern view relationships involve little more than isolated selves bumping up against one another. If our solitary selves can meet in a way that is mutually beneficial then it is labeled "a healthy relationship." But if that collision demands too much of my autonomy then you must be "co-dependent."

The basic problem with relationships according to modernity is that they so easily cause us to compromise our autonomy (call it sacrifice), to act in contradiction to our reason (call it love), or to bend our rational conclusions toward the constricting interests of others (call it empathy). Here's the crux: the existence of others, however close one may feel to them, must not change in any fundamental way who one is. Whether the other person exists or not has nothing to do with one's own selfhood. Being a self is simply given by virtue of the capacity to reason; it does not arise out of relationships—whether with other people or with God. Given this autonomous self—free from the infringements of God and neighbor—individuals may choose to be in mutually beneficial relationships. But it must be a free choice. And that choice to be in relationship does not in any way establish one's self-identity.

Early modern thinkers' suspicion surrounding relationships becomes intensified through the centuries. Descartes' distrust has been handed down to us in innumerable ways and in inflated forms. Perhaps the clearest echo of this distrust of relationships is expressed in a play by a twentieth century philosopher who is, interestingly, very much an heir of Descartes. Jean-Paul Sartre's *No Exit* is a play

about being trapped in Hell. Near the play's end the protagonist concludes: "Hell is—other people!"[2] If one listens carefully, one can hear
a late modern translation of Descarte's original triumphant conclusion: "I think, therefore I am." Sartre is right—on the underside of
autonomy is Hell. Autonomous existence confines others to Hell and
eventually reveals itself as Hell on earth for those who embrace it.

The Autonomous God

The most catastrophic consequence of the new understanding of the
self was a change in the view of God. Just as our relationships with
one another were redefined and marginalized within the confines of
autonomy, so also in the relationship with God. A rational affirmation of God's existence became more important than a personal,
trusting relationship. More specifically, in the philosophy of modern
thinkers such as Kant, we relate to God in the same way that we
relate to a principle with which we agree. If we agree with the principle that animals should be treated kindly, then we will attempt to
the best of our ability to treat animals kindly. In much the same way,
if we agree with the idea that God exists then we will live out the
implications of that idea day by day. For Kant these implications
consisted in a set of moral mandates.

Dangerously absent from this mindset is the sense that God
desires to live in a loving, trustful relationship with us. Believing in
God and assenting to the proposition that God exists are two very
different things. In the Bible faith is a trusting relationship with God,
not the affirmation that God exists—an affirmation, James would
remind us, that even the demons make (Jas. 2:19).

Beyond the diminishing of personal relationship with God, modern autonomy also redefined the understanding of God's nature
itself. History has proven that our views of ourselves always shape
our views of God. When we become autonomous, isolated selves,
God becomes an isolated subject. In such an environment the view
of God as a Trinity recedes. For such a view means that the Divine
Being is enmeshed in a set of relationships and, as we have seen,
relationships are the scourge of modern thinking. Descartes' axiom,

"I think therefore I am," thus casts its long shadow on the nature of God: God *is* because He thinks. God's nature, like ours, is reducible to His rational functions, rather than being defined by the limitless, expansive possibilities of love. Many moderns see God as a self-contained, autonomous and lonely rational agent removed from all those things that we experience but cannot account for rationally.

Indeed, because God is perfect He must possess a greater share of that autonomy than we do. To accomplish this act of making God supremely autonomous, He was often visualized as a set of rational principles, devoid of personal characteristics. In these accountings God is not the Covenant-Maker of Scripture but an entity to be rationally probed and admired for his strength and independence. Or perhaps, as with the Deists, God is a First Mover who set the universe in motion, designed scientific laws to govern the whole project, then rested in glorious isolation. For many, modernity marks the emphatic return of Aristotle's friendless god.

One's view of God need not be as radical as the Deists, however, to reflect the mindset of the modern, autonomous self. We see reflections of it in many Christian thinkers, not the least of which are Campbell and Fanning. For Campbell and Fanning God tends to become a subject to be researched through His book. Clues are extracted from that book, becoming data to be processed by our autonomous reason. In this process God does not compromise His autonomy by involving Himself personally in our lives. Instead, God has given us His book and through it He is accessible to our reason. Much like the Deists' claim that God set the universe in motion leaving His traces in scientific laws and then took a sabbatical, so also many of the Restorationists wrote as if God gave us the Word and then took a sabbatical.

The results of autonomy—ours and God's—have been well documented. We achieved a semblance of autonomy and control, but in the process left ourselves estranged from the very source of our lives. Loneliness and mediocrity ensued—but we are not without options.

The Relational Self

Autonomy is best understood as an obstacle to be overcome rather than a goal to be achieved. Autonomy neither defines our nature nor serves as the highest possibility for human fulfillment. To the contrary, through our relationships with one another and especially with God we become more fully human.

Consider the words of the author of Psalm 88 who, rather than celebrating, laments his autonomy. He complains of being in Sheol, "close to death," because he perceives the "Lord has cast Him off" and that he has become a "thing of horror to his companions." The psalmist suffers from a lack of identity, a living death, because of his isolation. He has no sense of self because he is cut off from his relationships. He feels trapped in Sartre's "no exit" situation, a suitably hellish metaphor for autonomy.

The notion that the self is autonomous and founded in its own ability to reason is actually a new idea. An older idea that is gaining precedence again in our age is that the self is created through relationships. The self is not a given based on reason, but the self is something that is always being gained, expanded and reshaped through our relationships. In other words, I am not a self by myself; I become a self in and through my relationships with others. We become who we are as we interact with other people, seeing ourselves a little differently through the eyes of others, and gaining more of an identity in a community of our peers. More particularly, as we learn to love others, to give of ourselves, to relinquish our pretensions to autonomy we come closer to being selves in the true sense of the word. Alone we are cut off from all the possibilities of what we can be, enslaved to our own sense of right and wrong, what is true and false. But in community we learn to see ourselves as part of a whole, with individuality to be sure, but an individuality that only comes alive in the midst of the whole.

This view of the self has been called the relational self, a name that explicitly contradicts the autonomous self. But we have only begun to explore it. Understanding ourselves as relational means that something, or actually someone, beyond our selves must be at work in us, making us into what we are intended to be. In other words, there must be an Other through whom we were created and are ever being recreated. The only Other with the creative potential to make us into selves is God, and it is our faith (trust) that allows Him to fashion us into His image.[3]

Becoming a self under God, becoming ruled by God rather than self-ruled, is not a one-time achievement. Rather, becoming a self is a continual process. Each day, each instant, we place our faith in God as He works within us. With each human relationship we enter, God gives us a new perspective on who we are. With each moment we are becoming selves, discovering new possibilities for our lives, new gifts and unprecedented horizons. These new possibilities and unprecedented horizons are very different from those promised by autonomy. They are not the "opportunities" for complete, self-absorbed self-rule. Quite the opposite: they are seen in moments when we find ourselves capable of sacrificial love in ways that we have never before dreamed possible. In these ways God is continually recreating us, molding us into perfect beings. Though we only see this continuing creation in part, we anxiously await the day when this new creation is complete.

The relational self assumes that our relationship with God is meant to be dynamic, ongoing, at once deeply personal and undeniably communal, but never static. This relationality can be sensed in much of Robert Richardson's theology, as when, for example, he describes faith as terminating not on the facts but "on the blessed Redeemer, realized subjectively in the inner-consciousness and spiritual affections of the soul." The word "subjectively" may give some reason to pause, but in the context of the argument it becomes clear that Richardson is describing God's work in creating us anew. "Subjective" here does not mean merely an interior opinion or fleeting emotion but rather a deep, mysterious, passionate and convicting union between Christ and us. Richardson's argument is that God is making us into something beautiful, something which if not immediately evident can at least be seen in our transformed dispositions and affections. More than that, we see God's work in moments of unreflective acts of love, in concrete acts of grace only possible because of God's working within us. These daily transformations may often feel tumultuous, but as the fruit of God's work is revealed there are moments of joy and ecstasy.

There is a doctrine that many Christians in the West have forgotten but that remains evident among Eastern Christians that describes the work God is doing. The doctrine describes God's work as a *theosis* or divinization of our natures.[4] In short the doctrine states that God, through his Spirit, is making us like Himself. We are in the process of becoming God-like. This doctrine does not suggest that we are taking God's sovereign place in the universe (as is often erroneously assumed); it simply states that God is creating a people with His own character. The doctrine of *theosis* affirms for Christians what Paul says about the world; God is in the process of becoming "all and all." We participate in God's becoming through faith; we catch glimpses of His work in our lives; and we learn to see our actions and attitudes as reflections of His own character.

But there is (as we have seen) much confusion about God's character and so we turn now to the second question: who is God?

The Trinity as God's Relationality

As we have seen, the way we think of ourselves has strong repercussions for the way we think of God. If in modernity the autonomous self created a God who lives in isolation from His creation, so the relational self sees God as living in relation with His community. In fact, the root of self-identity lies in God's work, not our own. Faith replaces reason as the instrument that allows us to receive and understand God's work. Whereas reason takes its point of departure from a human individual and returns to that human (in fact, it never really "gets off the ground"), faith begins as a response to the revelation of God's nature and rests solely upon the constancy of His Being.

A Biblical Overview of Human-Divine Relationships
More than placing relationality over modern autonomy or attempting to recast God in a more friendly human image, we are attempting to

affirm something very biblical here. Namely, everything we see, everything we think, even everything that we are is incomplete without God's intervention (Rom. 8:18-25). This means that God's activity alone maintains the universe, and that even in His constant care it will not be completed—it will continue to "groan"—until His Son returns.

As Christians, however, we are not simply waiting but also participating in God's future completion. For this reason the Bible describes our relationship with God in organic terms: we grow, mature and bear fruit because we are fed by a Source. When we speak of relationality we are suggesting that this growth and participation is not a process separate from the core of who we are. We do not have a nature or an identity and then participate in God's nature on top of what we already are. Rather, our participation in God's nature defines who we are; we become what He created us to be through our relationship with Him. Because of several factors (the existence of sin, the temptation to be autonomous, and simply because God is not finished with the world yet) becoming a self is something that awaits us, not something we already are. Nonetheless, we participate in our future identities in the present inasmuch as we commune with the living and personal God. This is a strange and complex notion and, indeed, it stands as a scandal to our stringent modern, reductive modes of thinking.

As strange as it sounds to those of us raised to believe in autonomy, being a self, according to Scripture, is a future hope instead of a present reality. Paul says as much when he tells the Colossians that our lives are "hidden with Christ in God" and will only be revealed when Christ "who is [our] life" is revealed (Col. 3:1-4). Our very identity, our "essence" (if you prefer), is inseparable from God's nature and will be fully revealed only in the future. This means that the only way for us to be fully human is for us to be in a pure relationship with God.

Paul makes it equally clear, however, that we catch glimpses of what we will be and, moreover, we are constantly growing into what we will be. The thrust of his message to the Colossians is to start being ("set your minds") now what you will one day fully be. This happens as we "grow up" into the head, Christ (Eph. 4:15-16). As 1 Corinthians 13 indicates, our faith (trust) in God initiates and maintains us in the process of becoming selves because it connects us with God. Faith allows us to see "in part" what we will one day see fully. While our faith is certainly imperfect, it will suffice until we no longer need faith, when we see God face to face. Until that time He leads us into ourselves, our true natures, through a trusting relationship with Himself and with others.

As the doctrine of *theosis* teaches us, our true nature is to be God-like. Again this notion is much less scandalous than it sounds to our modern ears. The question that this leads us to is, Who is God? What is the Divine character into which we were designed to grow? If Christ "is our life," if we are presently growing into our identity, what precisely is that identity?

A Biblical Overview of God's Relational Nature

The first thing to note is that God clearly is not the rational set of principles to which He has been reduced by many moderns. Throughout the Old Testament God is never conceived of as an object to be studied, scrutinized or proved. Instead, He is the God of covenant, the One who makes promises to people and receives in return their faithfulness. He rarely calls Himself "God," but usually reveals Himself either as "the Lord"—which implies a relationship with His subjects—or as "the God of Abraham, Isaac and Jacob." In other words, He is the God who is identified and known through His relationships, not a God known in isolation.

Throughout the Bible God also reveals His attributes, or better, His characteristics in personal and relational terms. God expresses emotions: He gets angry, shows compassion, declares love for His people in passionate and even romantic prose. God reveals Himself in such vivid personal and relational terms that it is at times almost uncomfortable for us to think of God in such ways.

Likewise, Jesus reveals the Father in relational terms. The "son of God" tells us to address his Father as "our Father" (Matt. 6:7-15). We are called the "children of God" and the "friends" of Jesus (John 15:14-15). The Spirit of God "inhabits" us as a "comforter" and seals us as God's children (John 14:23). As a result, God's Spirit forms us into "families" of believers who comprise the "body of Christ" (Eph. 4).

The relational language in which God reveals Himself is undeniable. Though God will occasionally use inanimate objects (a rock) or animals (an eagle) to identify one of His characteristics, in the overwhelming majority of cases He uses familial, personal and political terms. All of these are relational terms: they assume a prior relationship and express something within the parameters of a relationship. Scripture does not use abstract, non-relational and negative terms such as "infinite" (not finite), "impassible" (not emotional) or even "immutable" (not changeable) to reveal God's nature. These words are not only nonbiblical, but they easily distract us from the personal, positive and relational terms central in Scripture.

For many centuries, well before the advent of modernity, Christians wrestled with the relational language God uses to identify Himself. They actually came to something of a consensus regarding their uneasiness with the language, and it is a consensus that most of us have heard. The conventional wisdom is usually stated something like this: "God used such language metaphorically. He is not 'literally' Father, Son, Spirit or King. He does not really feel anger, pity, jealousy or love. He did not actually 'change His mind' for Abraham. He is beyond all such language. These are all mere concessions to our frail understanding." For the sake of clarity, we will call this the concessional view because it claims the relational language of Scripture is a concession to our understanding—it does not really portray who God is.

The circle of what can be taken seriously in the Bible's relational language is drawn in various ways. Some keep the relational terms "Father" and "Son" but throw out the gender implications of that language. Others dispense with all the emotions, labeling them as "mere concessions" (though inconsistently holding firmly to God's love). The basic problem is that the concessional view truncates or reduces much of the Biblical language about God. It claims that God cannot be defined in human terms even if that is how He reveals Himself because human rationality will not allow it.[5]

We face two choices here. Out of a desire to protect the distinction between God and human beings, we can affirm some hybrid form of the "concession" view. The assumption here is that simply because God reveals Himself in relational language does not mean that He is "in essence" relational. God can relate to us but with only a small piece of Himself. He is ensconced in some other realm to which we are not privy. He cannot be affected by time, cannot be hurt by our actions, cannot (really) change His mind, is not really bound to us by a covenant. God is free, which means that He does whatever He wants.

A second choice is to reject the concessional view and simply take the biblical language seriously. If the majority of the words and images God uses to reveal himself are relational, then we should assume that He is a relational Being. If John tells us that "God is love," and gives us no good reason to think that he is using hyperbole, then we should assume that God's nature at its core is love (1 John 4: 8). If Peter tells us that we can participate in that nature, then we should not read "between the lines" that he is actually saying we can participate in some small part of God's nature. Because God nowhere reveals Himself as a Being who can do whatever He wants, we should take Him at His word that He has entered into covenant with us, and that as a result He is "really" affected by the covenant relationship. God reveals Himself as inescapably relational. Any attempt to diminish that relationality fails to take seriously the very language God Himself uses.

Finally we have come full circle. On the one hand, many of the assumptions that have been handed down to us about God's nature are but fanciful images of our autonomous aspirations cast in the sky. God has never revealed Himself as autonomous or even as having some essence that is unaffected by His relationship with the creation. On the other hand, claiming that God is a relational or personal being is not a projection of ourselves onto His image if we take the Bible seriously. In fact, the revelation that we are relational beings stems from God's revelation that He is a relational Being. The language of the Bible is not primarily a concession to human understanding but rather an attempt to shape human understanding according to God's true nature.

But does the relational view endanger God's sovereignty? It need not if "sovereignty" is understood biblically. The distinction between us and God is the distinction between Father and children or a king and His people. More precisely, the primary difference between our nature and God's is that He will always be the perfect King and Father and we will always be less than perfect subjects and children. What establishes the distinction between parent/child or king/subject—what establishes God as sovereign over us—is not primarily His eternity, His immateriality or even His power. While these things all describe God in biblical terms, they tell us little about who He actually is. Knowing that God is eternal, knowing that He is invisible or knowing that He is almighty does not tell what sort of God He is. They describe some of His impressive qualities, but they get us no closer to some of the most basic questions about Him: Is He good or evil? What does He think of humans? Is He alone?

If we confess that God is sovereign because He is a perfect King and a perfect Father then we are also saying something very positive and specific about His nature. We are saying that all those things that make us good fathers and good authority figures are perfected in His nature. They are perfected because He relates to us as a perfect Father and a perfect King. What makes God the perfect Father and King are those things the Bible repeats over and over about His nature: He is holy, He is Love, He is good and He is faithful. These terms describe the character of God.

If we must speak philosophically then we would say God's essence is holiness, His nature is love, His transcendence is based in His goodness, He is infinitely faithful. There is no reason to claim that God's most essential part, His true nature, slips behind these very concrete, relational and personal descriptions. The most important distinctions between us and God are that He loves perfectly, we love imperfectly; He is holy, we are less than holy; He is good, we are not always good; He is ever-faithful to us, though we behave faithlessly toward Him.

In our discussion of the words Scripture uses to describe God, we are saying something quite simple: our God is perfectly relational and perfectly personal. He is perfect in all the qualities that enable us to have relationships.

From Relationality to the Trinity

We have been describing two opposing pictures of God, the concessional view and the relational view. The doctrine of the Trinity arose out of the clash between these two views. Something similar to the "concession" view gained prominence early in the history of Christianity. Influenced heavily by Greek dualism, many began claiming that God's essence lay beyond the reaches of time and relationships, and that the personal language in the Bible should not be taken too seriously. The doctrine of the Trinity was formulated in large part to defeat that mentality and to bring Christians back to a biblical, relational and personal understanding of God's nature.[6]

In much the same way, the doctrine has vanished and resurfaced at various times in the history of Christianity. The doctrine has been preserved in the liturgies of the classic Christian traditions, but its functionality, its ability to highlight the relational nature of God, has often waned when dualistic assumptions about God slipped into Christian thought. The modern period, with its brass heaven and all-pervasive notion of autonomy, has been particularly hostile to Trinitarian conceptions of God.

But around the middle of the twentieth century theologians and, more recently, ministers began rediscovering and reappropriating the Trinitarian doctrine. They claim to have found something in this classic doctrine that releases them from the spiritually anemic conditions of modernity. Something that allows them to experience God more fully. They are finding, in short, the very heart of what the Bible affirms about God's nature and personality.

The reasons for this return to the Trinity are not difficult to explain. Primarily, the Trinity is an attempt to affirm that God is a thoroughly relational being. The doctrine of the Trinity accents this truth by claiming that God not only forms relationships but that He is a relationship. Contrary to popular belief, this doctrine is not about how three can be one; it is not an attempt to obscure the clear teachings of the Bible about God. Certainly in its long history it has sometimes been presented that way, but this was not the intention of those who formulated it. Rather, the Trinity is a kind of shorthand summary continually directing us to the richness of God's relational nature revealed in Scripture.

The word "Trinity" is not used in Scripture, but the realities it illuminates about God are found all throughout Scripture. In the Bible we meet God as three different but unified Persons: the Father, the Son and the Spirit. (We call them "Persons" here not to diminish their Divinity but to recall the fact that the Bible reveals God in personal language.) At various times God identifies Himself with each Person: God reveals Himself as Father throughout both Testaments, God reveals Himself as the Son throughout the New Testament, and the Bible often refers to the Holy Spirit as the "Spirit of God." Each of these reveal themselves or, more properly, are revealed by one another as God. Scripture neither claims that one is more "God" than the others nor allows the possibility that there are three separate gods. Though the doctrine has caused intellectuals much consternation, the Bible has no concern to explain how this works out rationally or mathematically—how God is Father, Son and Spirit and still One. We simply have the witness of the biblical writers to God as Father, Son and Spirit yet one God.

Jesus and Paul offer us important clues as to how Father, Son and Spirit relate to each other. As we see especially in the Gospel of John, Jesus paints a picture of God's Being as a relationship between three Persons—a relationship so perfect, pure and intimate that "they" can only be called One. The love that binds them into one is manifest in the selfless way each reveals the other. Each points away from Himself and toward the Other. We see this repeatedly in the words of Jesus who emphasizes that his sole mission is to glorify his Father (John 12:28), who chastises a man who calls him "good" because

"God alone is good" (Mark 10:18), and who removes all doubt about his purpose by saying simply "if you have seen me, you have seen the Father" (John 14:9). At the same time Christ tells us that "all authority in heaven and on earth have been given to me [by the Father]" (Matt. 28:18). Paul tells us further that Jesus possesses the fullness of God's nature (Col. 1:19). Likewise, the Spirit is sent out to make Jesus present to the disciples (John 15:26), to continue the Father's work in the Body of Christ, and to make God Himself manifest to those who believe (2 Cor. 3:14-18).

The picture we get in Scripture is of a Divine community: three Divine Persons who are so perfectly related that they must be called One. Scripture makes no attempt to justify this oneness rationally. But it does indicate how we should think of God's unity. The oneness of God in the New Testament is a unity based in the self-giving love of the Father, Son and Spirit. Many texts bear this out, but the richest is the Philippian hymn, which we will examine in detail. These texts teach us that God is a unity of three Persons because each one divests Himself fully in the other. Each works to reveal the other perfectly: the Spirit points to the Son, as the Son directs us to the Father, who directs us back toward His empowering presence in the Spirit. Taken together—as "they" insist on being taken—"they" constitute One God, One Divine community unified in selfless devotion of each to the other.

Unity Created in Love

This Divine relationship is characterized by a unique type of love. It is this same love that flows out from God's nature and is poured into our own hearts. Philippians 2 best describes this process. One reason Paul writes the letter is to quiet the voices of contention in the church (Phil. 4:2). He is seeking to prevent internal strife and his method may strike us as odd: he points to the relational character of God. In fact, he quotes an ancient hymn that describes Christ as having "equality with God" but "emptying himself" of his nature for the sake of humanity. In return the Father "exalts" Christ "giving Him a name above all names."

Here we see the same selfless, mutual glorification between the Father and the Son that we described. But Paul also uses a specific word to describe the love intrinsic to God's nature: *kenosis.* This word is translated "self-emptying" and it lies at the core of the Trinitarian love. As Christ poured His life out (emptied himself) upon the cross, so also each member of the Trinity pours His Life out into the other. God's unique character is found in this self-emptying love.

God's love is not simply a self-love, though, nor is this self-emptying merely an emptying into God's own life. We must not forget Paul's purpose in quoting this hymn. Paul introduces it by telling the Philippians to "let the same mind be in you." Paul says that the character of Christians must be defined by the same self-emptying love seen in God's Life. We must not be about establishing ourselves, in ourselves, but of emptying ourselves into others. Paul is echoing the principle that was stated even more succinctly by Jesus: "those who find their life will lose it, and those who lose their life for my sake will find it" (Matt. 10:39).

But Paul is not simply telling Christians to use God's love as their example. Rather he is asserting that the self-giving love of God is "present" to us because God is at work in our lives. Paul does not say, simply, be like Christ or live up to this example, but "have the mind of Christ in you." He admonishes them to continue working out their salvation "because it is God who is at work in you, enabling you both to will and to work for His good pleasure" (2: 13). Paul gently reminds the Philippians that God's perfect love was available to them, a love that is at least strong enough to bind them into an unbreakable unity with one another and God.

Here we return to the Spirit's role in making us God-like. To become like God is to take on God's character, not to replace Him. That character is defined by *kenosis,* self-giving love. The unique role of the Spirit is to empty God's life into ours. In this way, God's relationality is opened for all of us to participate. "Participating in God's nature" is not an esoteric or mystical flight upward but a personal and communal experience of the self-emptying of God. Through such experiences we are transformed. The Spirit not only enables us to participate in God's nature, but He does so in order to recreate that same love in our relationships. We are transformed from self-absorbed, self-ruled individuals into self-giving agents of God's love.

This is the self which we are continually longing for, the self that we catch glimpses of in this life, but must await until the next for its completion. In this way we are not measured by our own versions of what we should be, but by our receptivity to God's indwelling Spirit. The life that John's gospel describes, the abundant life that is untarnished by death, is the life that flows from the nature of God into our lives.

What then do we hope to attain by using the word "Trinity?" In the broadest of strokes we can say that the Trinity summarizes the following biblical themes about God:

* God's relational nature;
* God's historical self-revelation as Father, Son and Spirit;
* The unique love that binds Father, Son and Spirit into a unity;
* God's movement toward us in the story of salvation, spanning from creation to consummation; and
* The way God's Life flows out to us—partially now and fully later.

When we affirm the doctrine of the Trinity we recall all of these biblical themes. More succinctly, the term "Trinity" is a human way of underscoring the fact that God's nature is such that we can "participate" in Him and He in us. Throughout the centuries use of the term "Trinity" has recalled this biblical fact about God's nature. This usage commends the term to us as a shorthand reminder of God's relational nature and self-giving character.

Because Christians are always tempted to lose sight of God's self-revelation as relational, personal and loving in Scripture, the doctrine of the Trinity, when understood correctly, functions to keep that revelation before us in all our endeavors. The doctrine of the Trinity disallows us from conforming our thinking about God to the world's thinking about Him. It does so by placing several excla-mation points after John's phrase, "God is love." In this way it serves as a vital reminder for Christians of every generation that we must be faithful to God's own way of describing Himself.

But it does even more. The doctrine also reminds us that God's relationality is not merely His own: we participate in the Trinitarian Life of God, and through His Spirit we begin to live in Trinitarian fellowship with one another. The expression "Trinitarian Life" not only describes God's nature but also the way His relational nature is partially realized in our relationships when seen through the eyes of faith. In the next chapter we will delve more deeply into the ways that the Trinity functions to help us experience God's relational Life.

Conclusion

In conclusion let us step back for a moment and contrast this vision of the self and God with the modern conception we have inherited in the main path of the Stone-Campbell movement. In that conception the self is defined by its ability to reason and is easily diminished by relationships. We discover God through the facts He has left behind in His Word; we "relate" to Him primarily by rationally assenting to, dwelling on and memorizing those facts. Under such conceptions God is often reduced to a set of intellectual principles, with our own faithfulness resting upon our ability to adhere to those principles.

In contrast, the less traveled path of the Restoration movement contains something of the relationality we have described. The self is gained, as Richardson claimed, in a "trusting relationship" with Jesus. The self is gained as we grow in faith, and our faith is increased by the work of the Spirit personally in our lives. To broad-en Richardson's vision: the more deeply we participate in God's Trinitarian Life, the more we take on His self-emptying character— and the more our true self takes shape. In short, as we participate in God's love we are enabled to love others with greater fervor and with fewer qualifications.

Here we find the solution to the postmodern crisis. We are not left abandoned, burdened with the impossible task of constructing ourselves by ourselves. Instead we are offered abundant Life, God's Life. Many of us have spent too long defying God's desire to create us anew, to create us in His image rather than He in ours. In this defiance we have reaped only fatigue, estrangement, even despair. Whether through the chaos of our times or the working of God, we are brought to a crisis, a crossroad. The crisis of postmodernity presents us with a new opportunity: we can turn into a new path and allow the breath of Life to fill our lungs once again, allow God to restore us in loving community, and let Him repel the demons of loneliness and self-reliance.

The urgency of our age also affords us the opportunity to refocus our tradition. In this age where people are seeking intimacy with a new urgency, we must seek to recover and reemphasize those essential elements of the Christian faith that receded or were eclipsed in the modern era. Our conviction is that the recovery of a more dynamic understanding of God's activity in our lives, found along a largely overgrown path in the tradition, can bring us new Spiritual vibrancy in a postmodern age.

Notes

1. Wolfhart Pannenberg, "The Christian Vision of God: The New Discussion on the Trinitarian Doctrine," *Asbury Theological Journal* 46 (Fall 1991), 28-29.

2. Jean-Paul Sartre, *No Exit and Three Other Plays* (New York: Vintage Books, 1946), 47.

3. The philosophical notion of the relational self with which we are working comes from the writings of the nineteenth-century Christian philosopher Soren Kierkegaard. For his explicit position see *The Sickness Unto Death.*

4. For an illuminating disscusion of this doctrine in relation to the Trinity and the Church in Eastern thought, see John D. Zizioulas, *Being as Communion* (Crestwood, New York: St. Vladimir's Seminary Press, 1985).

5. For a good treatment of the biblical anthropopathisms, see Terence E. Fretheim, *The Suffering of God: An Old Testament Perspective* (Philadelphia: Fortress, 1984).

6. For a comprehensive description of the origin of the doctrine of the Trinity in relation to the historical, social and philosophical climate, see Catherine Mowry LaCugna, *God for Us: The Trinity and Christian Life* (San Francisco: HarperCollins Publishers, 1991).

7

Trinitarian Life

I heard a preacher on the radio this morning who said: "God chooses to do whatever he wants. That's what makes Him God." I winced and shivered when I heard this. We have no desire to "put God into a box," and we recognize that God is more elusive than any of our concepts, but we also want to be faithful to the way He reveals Himself. Many biblical texts, such as Exodus 19:4-6 and Philippians 2:6-11, teach us that God desires to be in a relationship with His people and does so at the expense of the autonomy that is His by all rights. John's declaration that "God is love" teaches us why God wishes to be in a relationship with us. God's nature is love, a love so dramatic that He freely gives up His freedom to remain aloof from us and to do whatever He wants. In short, God remains true to Himself: He remains loving, faithful, good and holy even though that implies that He can be affected and effected by our actions.

This is our God's nature, but it is also the nature in which we are called to share. For this reason Paul tells Christians that they must give up their desire for autonomy, their desire to do whatever they want, in submission to God and out of love for one another (1 Cor. 9 and 10:23-33). Such a forfeiture is possible for us only because we partake of God's loving nature. It is this reality, this wonderful and

Spirit-empowered dynamic, that we refer to as Trinitarian Life. As the doctrine of the Trinity affirms that relational, covenantal love is inseparable from the very nature of God, Trinitarian Life highlights the way God's nature proceeds from His heart, through the cross and into our lives by the power of the indwelling Spirit.

In the following pages we will delve a little deeper into this mystery. Our emphasis, again, will not be on trying to make the Trinity make sense but rather on showing how this way of understanding God functions. We will do this by showing how it is able to inform our doctrinal choices and to shape the practices of the Church. And we will continue to point toward the Trinity as a doctrine that has everything to do with our Spiritual lives, not simply our intellectual lives.

A Doctrinal Framework for Experiencing God

Robert Richardson was haunted by the fear that the leaders of the "current reformation" had built a Temple that was largely empty. In other words, they had constructed a beautiful edifice by returning to Scripture, had restored the outward appearance of the first-century church and had done so with the right attitude. They had attempted to re-build the Church under the sole authority of the Bible. The problem was, according to Richardson, that they had not taken the Bible seriously enough. They used it as a guide, a building manual, but failed to take it seriously when it described how God inhabits His Temple and how we can encounter Him there. In other words, they—and many of us—constructed a biblical Temple but it has "yet to be filled with the Divine Presence" as the Bible promises. Richardson's conclusion about the absence of the promised Divine presence was not that God is unfaithful but that many closed themselves off to that possibility.

Instead, Richardson claimed, many restorers became preoccupied with the dimensions of the Temple itself, the architecture and the tools of construction. Indeed, the Temple was impressive and its construction was quite a feat, but the mere construction of the Temple was not the goal. Its existence serves a function, to house the Spirit of God, and until it serves that function it stands only as an empty temple.

To switch metaphors, N. T. Wright has compared the structure of the Bible to a Shakespearean play. He argues that there are five acts to the Bible, with each act consisting of five different scenes. Act One was Creation; Act Two was the Fall; Act Three was the Exodus and the history of Israel; Act Four was the Incarnation of Jesus Christ; and Scene One of Act Five was the writing of the New Testament and the disclosure of how the play ends. The rest of Act Five is us, the Church.[1] In other words, we are presently living out the Biblical narrative in our everyday lives. We are the Church, the Church that began at Pentecost, has continued to this very day and continues only by the grace of God.

Central to Act Five, to our present situation, is an extremely important turn of events that occurred after the Resurrection of Christ. The Spirit of God has come upon us, imbued us with His transform-ing power, and stays to ensure that the play will not end as a tragedy or a farce. The importance of this turn of events cannot be exagger-ated, indeed, it is the fundamental conviction and experience that shapes our Christian identity.

If we merge these two metaphors, we may be able to see the importance of the Spirit's role more clearly. Our lives look fairly vac-uous, meaningless and insignificant if we believe that all Christianity is about is visiting an empty temple a few times a week. Our lives look just as empty if we see ourselves as actors merely mimicking a two-thousand-year-old play that many of us have known by rote since we can remember. If Christianity is just about mouthing the words to a beautiful play or sanding off the rough edges in a sub-lime yet empty temple then there is little value in it—save that of warding off fears about the "undiscovered country." Yet Christianity is always threatened by this possibility. Such a reduction offers little hope in this life, little sense of the meaningfulness and splendor that was experienced by Christians in the Bible itself.

On the contrary, if Christianity is about a Temple filled with God's Presence and about ourselves as temples housing the Spirit of God, things begin to look quite different. If we see our lives not as "living up to" a set of standards but the active "living out" of the drama of Scripture, we get quite a different picture. Suddenly the Christian Life looks more luminous, more inviting, more open and more significant. Our experiences are no longer removed from our faith in God, rather they become assimilated in the Biblical drama of salvation, recast in the knowledge and awareness of God's indwelling. Through many of our experiences we are able to see unforeseen dimensions in God's drama, locate new arenas of Kingdom Life, understand these as God's artistic expressions (Eph. 2:10) and, at times, feel a portion of God's sadness. But all of these experiences take on eternal significance. They are not merely swept aside as irrelevant and meaningless but instead become the conduits of God's Presence in our everyday lives.

In a simple word, this discussion of Trinitarian Spirituality is meant to help us see our lives as meaning-full, indeed, for us to see ourselves not so much as foot soldiers following Divine orders but as active partakers of the Divine Nature. God's plan throughout Scripture points to our age, to Act Five, as the age where He becomes deeply involved in our lives and we become deeply involved in His. The writer of Hebrews reminds us that generations of Godly people longed to see our day (Heb. 11:39-40). But in a strange and tragically ironic twist many of us have erected barriers to this involvement by something as seemingly innocuous as a few bad ideas. Others of us have been victimized by the fact that those barriers were erected in the first place. These barriers are high and we should not take them lightly, but they are not insurmountable.

Specifically, when we understand our lives as self-governed or autonomous, and see God as an autonomously reigning, distant Monarch, the Christian life slowly begins to get distorted. When these ideas take hold, sink in deeply, God's Presence is blocked by our expectations. Ironically, this in itself is proof that we can affect God and that, whether we like it or not, we are in a deep relationship with Him. If we want God at a distance, with enough practice and time, we can in fact force Him from us. In the same way, if we become preoccupied with the dimensions of the Temple and the choreography of the play, so much so that we forget that the Temple only exists and the play only goes on so that we can partake of His Life, then indeed He will seem distant. To an extent God will be for us what we think He is—even if we think Him an abstract monarch who has left us some impossible rules to live up to and taken a hiatus. The point is that if we insist on understanding ourselves as autonomous beings and God as a supremely perfect autonomous Being then this can become the only option for the Christian Life.

The doctrine of the Trinity is a way to get us past these ideas, indeed, to shatter them. It is not a magical formula, and it is not a panacea to all Spiritual and doctrinal ailments. Rather it is a useful, conceptual tool for avoiding certain dangers and for beginning with a clear focus on God's revelation of Himself. If we begin immediately with the confession that God is a community of persons so defined by self-giving love that He is rightly called One, then all notions of autonomy are excluded. If we go further and say that we also are not autonomous, though we are tempted to live autonomously, then we can begin to get a sense of a Life that is permeated by God Himself. Instead of "living up" to a Divine standard issued from a remote and impersonal "thinking thing," we see our lives, individually and as a church, intimately involved with the unfolding of God's plan. Instead of seeing our goal as perfecting an empty Temple by merely restoring belief "in" the New Testament, we are able to see our lives as filled yet imperfect temples, acting to restore the beliefs "of" the New Testament. Indeed, we are able to see ourselves not merely as actors repeatedly mouthing their lines but as participants and co-heirs of a Kingdom that is coming in the present.

We tend to think that ideas, especially those that seem unfamiliar such as the doctrine of the Trinity or modern autonomy, do not affect our lives in any practical way. One of the most inescapable truths of history is that ideas do affect our everyday lives in dramatic if not always obvious ways. Ideas, good ones and bad ones, affect how we live in more ways than any of us know.

Perhaps the best analogy is to think of our ideas as a field of vision. Anyone who has suffered from myopia can testify to the way that disease shapes, reduces and distorts their perceptions of the world. Because peripheral vision is blocked, a person with this disease can often see only what is right in front of his face. If something happens just to either side of his fixed gaze the person completely misses it and is forced to rely on someone's report. That report may be accurate or inaccurate, but whatever the case it cannot take the place of the experience of seeing itself. Because the person's vision is limited, he misses many of the normal experiences many of us take for granted.

Ideas function in a similar way. The way we think of the world, ourselves and God shapes what we see and do not see. This is especially true of ideas that we do not even recognize in ourselves. Someone with myopia may become so accustomed to it that she may be able to function with a great deal of efficiency in spite of her limitations. Similarly, our ideas inform our way of experiencing the world, our way of interpreting our experiences and, indeed, even condition which experiences we are able to have. We become accustomed to the process, we quit noticing that portions of life are filtered out by our ideas, and we function in the world accordingly. Our ideas, especially those that we are unable to articulate, inform the way we "see" the world and the way we "see" Scripture. They are the expectations which separate the possible from the impossible, forming the borders of our lives.

Many of us, even all of us to some extent, suffer from a theoretical myopia. From the time we entered this world we have been indoctrinated by ideas that have steadily and consistently eroded our range of vision. From commercials, to political speeches, to classrooms, we have been told that our greatest goal in life is to be independent of others. Autonomy has been dangled before us as who we are and who we are to become. To add to this, many of us who have grown up in church traditions shaped by modernity have had our vision further truncated. The ideas ingrained in us have been set deep in our consciousness, so much so that long after we have rejected notions that God is a lonely King, that we are lonely subjects and that our only way to experience Him is through a rational collection of the words of the New Testament, our expectations are still sharply delimited. Because we do not expect God to move in certain ways, because we think that we cannot hear His voice in our daily experiences we, of course, do not "see" any of this. In this way, an idea as seemingly abstract and distant as the cry of a seventeenth-century philosopher—"I think, therefore I am"—exerts a tremendous influence on our daily lives.

Faced with our theoretical myopia, we have a few options, all of which will cost us something. We can take succor in our myopia and quell the desires of our own hearts for something more rich, dynamic and meaningful. If we choose this route, we would not be alone. In fact, Christian bookstores are overflowing with guides to preserving this sort of myopia. There is, alas, a wealth of such material published by the "defenders of the truth" in the Stone-Campbell movement—though we would argue that key parts of the "truth" that they defend are only a couple of hundred years old. Myopia can be comforting and there is always money to be made in comforting others who refuse to grow. But there is also much to lose: the Christian life will continue to be thin, passionless and mainly a waiting for the next life.

Another option is to replace the ideas we have inherited with other ideas. It might seem that we are proposing this option by replacing the "dirt philosophy" and autonomy with the Trinity and relationality. But if ideas readily function to reduce our vision, then this would only be replacing one form of myopia for another form of the same disease. Though a fresh look at the world is refreshing, eventually the same limitations would beset the new vision. Our claim is a bit more audacious than that. We recognize that any idea, even a good one like the Trinity, contains the potential for becoming a new myopia. We will deal with some practical ways that the Trinity keeps us from a one-sided, overly ossified and incomplete version of Christian life in the next section. First it is important that we indicate, in a more theoretical way, what precisely we intend to accomplish by focusing on relationality and the Trinity.

Since we cannot rid ourselves of ideas altogether (nor should we try), the only other option is to have ideas with holes in them. This is of course a scandal to our stringent, inherent rationalism—and it should be. The doctrine of the Trinity, properly conceived, is a loose or open idea, one that lays out some basic, biblical parameters about who God is (and who we are) with the expectation that God will fill in the gaps himself. In other words, to speak of ourselves as relational beings and God as the perfect Relational Being is to say that at the heart of our existence and God's lies a Divine mystery (another scandal for modernity).

Mystery here does not mean we have arrived at an impasse or that we are simply saying, "I don't know." Mystery rather is the gaping hole in our ideas about God through which God moves into our lives, ceasing to be simply an idea. It is not the sort of mystery that leaves us mired in indecision, but instead is a transformative awakening to the mystery in whom "we live, move, and have our very being" (Acts 17: 28). Most ideas (especially modern ideas) begin by expelling mystery, by closing off everything into a tight circle of reason and logical consistency, and by arresting the movement, the potential distractions from outsiders. With the doctrine of the Trinity we are after another sort of idea, one which begins by saying that we live inside of a mystery that yields meaning, one which recognizes truth is a person instead of a rationally-consistent proposition, and one which welcomes and seeks the distractions caused by the arrival of an outsider. The idea of the Trinity is an arrangement of basic biblical themes about God designed to allow God Himself to animate and demonstrate those themes in our lives.

Essentially then this talk of relationality—ours and God's—is a way of clearing out bad ideas (autonomy and sensualism), ushering in some key biblical insights (the Kingdom of God, the presence of the Spirit), and opening ourselves for deeper experiences of God in the present. This last notion is the most difficult and potentially disconcerting. But in reality it is nothing more than saying that God is more like a person than an idea. When we think of God apart from His relationships, we are treating Him in a way that is more like an idea than a person. We would never dream of treating our friends or spouses apart from our relationship with them. We cannot fully describe a friend to someone; we cannot expect anyone to "know" the "essence" of our friend from such a description. We would not reduce our friends to impersonal ideas because we recognize that they are too deeply immersed in our lives and are of themselves too dynamic to be contained in a set of rationally-conceived, logically-consistent principles. Why would we expect God to be otherwise? How can we expect to know Him apart from our relationship with Him? For this very reason the Bible reveals God as our Father, not as an "unmoved mover" or "first principle."

In fact, we affirm something very biblical (and very unphilosophical) when we affirm God's relational nature. We affirm that God is the God of Abraham, Isaac, Jacob and Jesus. We affirm that He is a God who makes covenants. We affirm that God has called us into a relationship that defines not just what we think, not just how we live, but who we actually are. In short, we affirm that the work of creation is not done, is still being done, as we are ever formed into the New Creation that God intends.

We introduced this section as a "doctrinal framework for experiencing God." It is time to explain that. What we have sought to do here is to lay the broadest possible framework for allowing God to be Himself in our lives. Our claim has been that we have imposed narrow, myopic restriction upon God, that under the influence of modernity we have made God something He is not. We have done this by forcing Him from an active and dynamic participation in our lives into a mere "objective idea" or a distant lawgiver.

When we say that God is relational we are identifying His fundamental nature. We are saying that above all God desires a relationship with us, desires to form us into His Image, to make us new. At the same time, we are saying that the ways in which God does this, apart from the biblical guidelines, cannot be codified into a simple program. If we confess with Scripture that God is bigger than any of our ideas about Him, then the first step in getting to know Him is to disallow our ideas from defining Him too rigidly. Instead, we must attempt to allow God to define Himself for us by opening our minds and our hearts to a world that is robust and pulsating with His Presence. In short, to begin to understand God we must understand that the Temple is still being filled, that the drama of salvation continues, and that we have a crucial and active part in that drama.

How the Trinity Keeps the Church on Track

As we saw at the beginning of the last chapter, the doctrine of the Trinity is not about some strange heavenly arithmetic that theologians like to play with. We care hardly at all for such games. The doctrine rather is a kind of shorthand for referring to what we know of God now that Jesus has come (Incarnation) and the Spirit has been poured out (Pentecost). It serves an extremely vital function: it keeps us clear about which God we are talking about—not Aristotle's god, not Plato's god, not the god of modern Deism, not the god of Deepak Chopra; but the One who revealed himself supremely in the earthly life of Jesus Christ and whom we now experience through the presence of the Spirit. And we desperately need the clarity. For we are prone constantly to forgetfulness and to a great variety of distortions.

Many gods are worshipped in our culture. The pollsters who try to find out how many Americans believe in God usually do not ask, "Which one?" But that is the more relevant and important question these days. The spiritual hunger and searching of our time—the collapse of the brass dome over the heavens—has reopened the pantheon of gods and goddesses. People everywhere are becoming believers— but in many strange gods. A whole range of neo-paganisms mark the now fertile spiritual landscape of postmodern culture.

When the early church entered into its long conflict with paganism, the central question at the heart of the conflict was always, "Who is God?" The answer to this most basic question was, finally, the doctrine of the Trinity. Faced with the might and allure of paganism, its formulators were trying to hold onto and make explicit the central pattern of truth about God in Christian Scripture. Faced again with the pressure and allure of paganism, as we are now, the doctrine of the Trinity must again be rethought, reclaimed and pressed into service.[2] And indeed such recovery is well under way through the rich and creative work of devout theologians from a variety of Christian traditions.

Not only is this doctrine a key element in the new face-off with paganism, it is a key tool for keeping churches themselves healthy and on track. Though a rich mystery, the Trinity is a crucially practical doctrine—practical in the sense that it fundamentally shapes our practices as Christian communities. For the way we understand God's manner of loving and relating to people sets the pattern for how God's followers conduct their life together and carry out their ministry to the world.

So we turn now to examine some of the ways Trinitarian doctrine functions to check the many distortions and imbalances to which Christian life is prone. Put in Trinitarian terms, Christian Spirituality means following the risen Christ, in the power of the Spirit, to the glory and praise of the Father. Each of these three truths provides a check against serious and common distortions of the Christian way.

Following the Risen Christ
The Spiritual life, whatever else it may be, is a life of obedience and discipleship. It means taking up the cross and following Jesus, walking in his way of loving and serving, his way of treating enemies, his way of giving and forgiving. It means, in short, imitating Jesus. It involves training in self-renunciation, counting the cost, renouncing lordship over people and gaining a new attitude toward money and possessions. It is an external, visible, very concrete path of obedience and sacrifice.

This focus of the Spiritual life is a check against triumphalism, Spiritual elitism, authoritarianism and experientialism. Triumphalism claims that resurrection life has superceded life under the cross, that the Christian life is a life of uninterrupted bounty, success and triumph. Its close cousin, Spiritual elitism, claims that possessing certain Spiritual gifts and powers places one on a higher Spiritual plane, well above the ordinary believer. Both claims are common—ranging all the way from Corinth to cable TV. But standing against both is the call to cruciform discipleship, to follow Jesus in the way of sacrificial love.

Authoritarianism is the fleshly desire to control, manipulate and lord it over people, variously exercised under the claims of Divine anointing, Kingdom efficiency and Scriptural precedent. The way of Jesus always says No. "I am among you as one who serves," he says—and takes up the basin and the towel. Spiritual experientialism is the hankering after miraculous visitations and the running after supernatural sensations, the seeking of one spiritual thrill after another. To this, Jesus says, "Come, follow me. Love your neighbor as yourself. Feed my sheep. As much as you did it unto the least of these, you did it unto me." The call to follow Jesus is always a call to obedience, to faithful burden-bearing, to patient endurance, to forgiveness and tangible acts of love.

In the Power of the Spirit

The Spiritual life, whatever else it may be, is a life indwelt and empowered by the Spirit of God. For Paul the term "spiritual" refers specifically to the life produced by the presence and work of the Holy Spirit (thus "Spirit-uality," not the vague, psychologized "spirituality" of contemporary usage). The Spirit is basically God's Presence in power/weakness among God's people. The Spirit dwells in Christians—indeed can fill us—and the location of that indwelling is the "heart" (2 Cor. 1:22; 3:3; Gal. 4:6; Rom. 2:29; 5:5). The Spirit is the source of transformation and Christ-likeness in disciples, the very Life of God coursing in us and through us.

This focus of the Spiritual life is a check against moralism, legalism, rationalism and Bible deism. Without the Spirit, discipleship, with its stress on obedience, sacrifice and righteousness, quickly becomes moralistic and legalistic. Moralism is the confidence that we can get better and better if we will just try harder and harder. And legalism—a natural and constant human propensity—reduces relationship to rule-keeping. The Spirit counters all moralism and legalism by inviting us into the intimacy and joy—even ecstasy—of the Divine Life, indeed, by being the bearer of that Life.

Rationalism, as we have seen already, treats God more as an idea or rational principle than a person, thus diminishing or even denying true relationality. And Bible deism, which is a form of rationalism, confines our relationship with God to ingesting the words of the Bible. Against both, the focus on the power and presence of the Spirit upholds the personal, experiential and intimate character of life with God.

To the Glory and Praise of the Father

The Spiritual life, whatever else it may be, is a life devoted to the glory of God and the coming of His Kingdom. At the heart of the biblical story is the mighty Creator God, the maker of heaven and earth, the One who sustains the world and human life in it. He is personally and passionately involved in the created order but totally distinct from it, never to be identified with the forces of nature. He is the elusive transcendent One who will not be domesticated or brought under human control. The created order is a theater of His glory, and human life finds its proper end in the praise of God.

This focus of the Spiritual life is a check against all idolatries, magic and domestication of the faith. Idolatry is a constant human temptation, for we are creatures prone, at every moment, to fashion God in our own image. Scripture makes clear that idolatry, at its core, is a religious disguise for self-centeredness. Idols are projections of the human will. They represent attempts to make God less transcendent, less elusive, less sovereign and free, more at the beck and call of human interests. The practice of magic is a close corollary. Magic is the attempt to manipulate God or the gods through the use of "automatic" techniques like incantations, spells, sacred objects and the like. It is blatant and frightening when it appears in black magic and the occult; but it takes much more subtle form when Christian practices and beliefs get recast as "automatic" techniques to summon or control God. Focus on God the Father resists the powerful and deep human impulse to bind God to human agendas through idolatry and magic. It enables us to critique and resist the domestication of God in the service of personal, economic and social interests.

Returning to Sound Doctrine

God leads a relational life as Father, Son and Spirit. That life is characterized by submissive love, as each member of the Trinity pours His life into the other. In God's own self there is an abundant outpouring of life, so abundant that it overflows and creates community with God's creatures—those outside the relationship within God. Through the sending of the Son and the outpouring of the Spirit, God shares this rich life with His creatures. As Diogenes Allen puts it: "The life of the Trinity is a perfect community and it is the kind of community for which we long; it satisfies our craving to be loved perfectly and to be attached to others properly."[3]

The Christian faith invites people to receive—to experience—this Life. But in a focused way: through Jesus Christ and the truth of his Word. The living God longs for His creatures to participate in the Divine Life—the richest life of all—and to know Him personally and enjoy Him. The doctrine of the Trinity is the essential doctrinal framework guiding and protecting such experience. It provides focus and boundaries. It counters both rationalism and narcissistic experientialism, both grim legalism and spiritual self-indulgence. Against the steady pull of deism (God aloof and distant) and domestication (God harnessed to personal agendas), sound Trinitarian doctrine upholds the wonderful mystery of a God who shares His life intimately with us but who will not be contained by any of us. And for a tradition without language to speak of encountering, experiencing and enjoying God, it provides the language.

In becoming more fully Trinitarian in practice, Churches of Christ especially face the challenge of developing a Trinitarian doctrine of the Holy Spirit.[4] Here the barriers of tradition remain high and forbidding. Here the long reach of the "dirt philosophy" remains most firmly felt. Yet after the fall of the brass heaven, as we have seen, the atmosphere is more hospitable precisely at this point. After several centuries of being desacralized, the world is being resacralized. The world of things unseen is becoming less and less foreign to more and more people.

In postmodern culture, in fact, the challenge becomes, not so much creating openness to spiritual reality and experience, but rather constraining and disciplining it so that believers' lives are conformed to the way of Jesus and the practices of God's Kingdom. Trinitarian doctrine is our chief tool for constraining and focusing the spiritual effulgence of a resacralized world that will always be prone to spiritual narcissism and illusion. As Eugene Peterson has well said, "Contemporary spirituality desperately needs focus, precision, and roots: focus on Christ, precision in the Scriptures, and roots in a healthy tradition."[5] But on a different front, Trinitarian doctrine is also our chief tool for opening up believers to the power and presence of the living God when they have constricted that reality through accommodation to modernity.

So the challenge becomes, both for Churches of Christ (who have overly minimized that reality) and for some other churches (who have, at times, overly magnified it), to recover a discipleship rooted in a Trinitarian doctrine of the Spirit. Christian discipleship involves following the risen Lord, in the power of the Spirit, to the glory of the Father and the coming of His Kingdom. In the Trinitarian economy the present work of the Spirit is primarily eschatological. That is, the Spirit, using means that are finite and contingent, anticipates and makes real the life to come in the present life of the Christian community. Full and faithful discipleship, then, is supernatural or Spirit empowered; believers walk in a way and engage in practices that are humanly impossible but that in the power of the Spirit become possible. When discipleship is not rooted in the Spirit's power it gets tamed or toned down to what seems humanly possible, simply reasonable and culturally appropriate.

Certainly in their congregations members of Churches of Christ have experienced the Spirit's empowerment to various degrees—they have sought to practice Christ's ordinances faithfully, have learned to pray and have sought to love and serve one another and the weak; but their doctrine has not adequately accounted for or supported this experience and their language has not adequately named it. Further, their worship has lacked Trinitarian language and shape. This doctrinal deficiency has inhibited and often distorted practice. Legalism and moralism have flourished.

Standing at this present crossroad, Churches of Christ need to recover a fuller, more practical Trinitarian faith to correct and refocus their doctrinal and liturgical tradition. Gordon Fee, gathering up the fruit of his extensive exegesis of all the Spirit texts in Paul, has put this recovery in terms that can resonate with Churches of Christ: "a genuine recapturing of the Pauline perspective will cause the church to be more vitally Trinitarian, not only in its theology, but in its life and Spirituality as well. This will mean not the exaltation of the Spirit, but the exaltation of God; and it will mean not focus on the Spirit as such, but on the Son, crucified and risen, Savior and Lord of all."[6]

There is much more that needs to be said about recovering Trinitarian Life in our movement. The notion of relationality requires changes in some of our practices and conceptions of the Christian faith. The way we do church, the priority we give to living in the last times, our understanding of and openness to the Spirit, and our understanding of evangelism are just a few examples. We believe that God is moving us in a new direction—a direction that is not new to Him and should not be new to us but that years of forgetfulness make seem new. In this postmodern season where the future looks bleak and the present feels so disorienting, God is bringing us into new levels of intimacy with Himself and one another.

Notes

1. N. T. Wright, *The New Testament and the People of God: Christian Origins and the Question of God: Volume 1* (Minneapolis: Fortress Press, 1992), 140-142.

2. Wright, *Bringing the Church to the World*, 204-207.

3. Diogenes Allen, *The Path of Perfect Love* (Cambridge, MA: Cowley, 1992), 52. This is one of the best discussions of God's relational life and how that life creates community with human beings. See pp. 39-59.

4. Over a decade ago Albert Outler spoke of the urgent need for "an updated pneumatology that includes historical perspective along with the opening horizons

of a postmodern and global age." Significant works attempting to do this include: Killian McDonnell, "A Trinitarian Doctrine of the Holy Spirit," *Theological Studies* 46 (1985), 191-227; Jurgen Moltmann, *The Spirit of Life: A Universal Affirmation* (Philadelphia: Fortress, 1992); and Clark Pinnock, *Flame of Love: A Theology of the Holy Spirit* (Downers Grove, IL: InterVarsity, 1996).

5. Eugene Peterson, *Subversive Spirituality* (Grand Rapids: Eerdmans, 1994, 1997), 36.

6. Gordon Fee, *God's Empowering Presence: The Holy Spirit in the Letters of Paul* (Peabody, MA: Hendrickson, 1994), 902. See also his more popular treatment of Trinitarian pneumatology in *Paul, the Spirit, and the People of God* (Peabody, MA: Hendrickson, 1996), 36-48.

Conclusion

Needed now is training in being more functionally Trinitarian—training which happens best in worship. We need exercises to instill in us a fuller consciousness of the relational nature of our God—the wonderful vision that God's own Life embodies the kind of love in relationship that we long for in our deepest longings.

8

On the Road

The journey we have described in this book has been long and challenging. We began with the crossroad represented by the 1857 debate between Robert Richardson and Tolbert Fanning in order to demonstrate the depth of modernity's influence on our tradition. We then moved to the present crossroad, where society at large is taking issue with the modern ideology that has deeply shaped our tradition, especially with its failure to nurture intimacy. We suggested that these challenges require us to focus on the less traveled path which from the beginning was at odds with modernity. We claimed that preserving the central tenets of our tradition—separating them from the restrictive influence of modernity and rounding out the less traveled path—was possible and vital if Churches of Christ are to withstand the crisis of postmodernity. Finally, we attempted to round out that path by pointing toward a relational view of the self and a Trinitarian view of God which, when combined faithfully, constitute a biblical vision of Trinitarian Life.

We turn finally to the road ahead. How can we move forward at this present juncture? What steps can redirect our practices and deepen our vision? How can we participate more richly in God's Life?

An Idiot's Guide to Being Trinitarian?

In Chapter 5 we discussed the many dualisms that beset modern thinking, fragment the Western worldview and splinter our lives. Among these, and one of the most enduring and pervasive, is the dualism between the theoretical and the practical. This dualism is expressed in virtually every facet of American culture including the curricula of most Christian institutions of higher learning. Many Christian universities require their students of religion to take certain "systematic theology" courses that are followed by a series of "practical theology" courses. The idea is that one learns conceptual knowledge about the Christian faith and then the same conceptual knowledge is "made practical." The reality is quite different: invariably students complain that the theology courses offer little guidance in daily ministry and, conversely, that the practical courses contain insufficient theological or even Christian insight. The result is frustration, even a sense of helplessness, before the deep gulf that separates theory from practice.[1]

One need not be or have been a theology student, however, to feel the same sense of frustration or helplessness. A glance through one of the mega-bookstores confirms that this same rift between theory and practice characterizes other disciplines and fields of study. The main bridge between theory and practice seems to be the array of "Idiot Guides" displayed prominently on the selves. On the one hand, the public cries for knowledge that is relevant, practical and methodical. On the other, academics and scientists insist with equal fervor that knowledge maintain its theoretical purity and scientific rigor at all cost. As a result most of us have become repositories of two kinds of knowledge: knowledge that is so practical it is nearly meaningless and knowledge so esoteric that it has little value.

Now we, the authors, face a similar dilemma. Shall we conclude with an "Idiot's Guide to Becoming Trinitarian"? Or shall we take our stand on the high principle of irrelevancy? We wish to do neither. Though this book is indeed quite theoretical, it has been written from different convictions than those which establish this dualism in the first place.

How then are we to conclude? We will list some practice-orienting conclusions, some "steps on the road." But these should not be read as an all-encompassing method for a recovery of the Divine Presence. Such an intention would itself be a wholesale concession to modernity. Instead, we offer up the conviction that has undergirded and shaped this project: overcoming autonomy and overcoming the dualisms of modernity is the work of God, not our own.

Neither the most profound of thoughts nor the most efficient of methodologies can accomplish this great feat. Certainly we can impede God's work with our bad ideas and counter-productive practices, but He still finds ways of penetrating them. God fills the abysmal gulf between our theories and our practices. God animates our lives in spite of our lifeless thinking. God moves into our thoughts even if they seem overcrowded with the "to-do" lists of our lives. But we often miss God's best work because we are not intellectually focused on His mysterious Presence or Spiritually attuned to His rhythmic and sometimes surprising movements.

As a culture and as a church tradition we are often unfocused and unattuned. This problem is neither a theoretical one, though it can receive elaborate theoretical expressions, nor a practical one, though it certainly has immense practical ramifications. It is simply a problem, and a messy and complicated one at that. Likewise the best way out of the problem lies neither in getting our thinking straight nor in finding the most efficient methodology. The problem is a spiritual one because spiritual forces are at work in the problem itself. The cure is likewise Spiritual because only God Who Is Spirit can bring us kicking and screaming out of modernity.

Thus even if we had all the theoretical resources and practical insight at our disposal, we cannot simply say "this is how to become Trinitarian" any more than we can say "this is how to fall in love." Instead, we call on God in conclusion, not as a last-ditch effort because theory and practice have failed us, but as a first effort because the forces that confront us are spiritual/Spiritual in nature and beyond human manipulation.

Steps on the Road

1. Learning to enjoy God.

This step will no doubt sound strange to many devoted Christian ears. Study God, yes. Obey God, certainly. Sacrifice for God, of course. But enjoy God? How odd.

For many churchgoers the Christian way has been taught and modeled as basically a solemn, if not grim, duty. God was the stern lawgiver, perhaps even the harsh taskmaster. Fear, respect and obedience were the appropriate responses. Delight and enjoyment were reserved for more mundane affairs—and may have remained a bit suspect even there. True religion, after all, means curtailing or suppressing the powerful human desire for pleasure, for it is this very desire that opens the door to much triviality and carnality.

Given these common religious reflexes, C. S. Lewis startles us a bit when he says that the problem is not that our desire for pleasure is too great but that it is far too small. "We are half-hearted creatures," Lewis says, "fooling about with drink and sex and ambition when infinite joy is offered us, like an ignorant child who wants to go on making mudpies in a slum because he cannot imagine what is meant by the offer of a holiday at the sea. We are far too easily pleased."[2] Surprising too perhaps is the Psalmists repeated admonition to "Delight yourself in the Lord!" (Ps. 37:4).

As we have seen in the last two chapters, at the heart of Trinitarian Life is the perfect love shared between the Father, the Son and the Spirit. Not only is that love sacrificial and unselfish, it is also full of joy and delight. It is Life indeed, the kind of life we seek in our truest and deepest desires—the inconsolable longing within us. When we experience it or glimpse it, we know it is what we were made for and what we long for more than anything else. At the heart of the Christian faith is the astounding truth that God seeks to share that Life with us, to invite us, indeed to draw us, into the fellowship of that Life, to experience its delight and joy.

In worship, when we praise and make melody to the Lord we can begin to experience on this earth the joy of God's own Life in heaven. Worship basically flows out of adoration, and we adore only what delights us. We adore only what fills us with joy.[3] Praise then becomes what flows out of our adoration.

Becoming more functionally Trinitarian will mean, at the heart of Christian experience and practice, learning to enjoy God, to enter into the love, delight and blessedness of God's own Life.

2. Employing exercises for building Trinitarian consciousness.

Churches of Christ, in their relatively brief modern history, have chosen a path of isolation and separation from the great stream of historic Christian orthodoxy. They chose this path, for the most part, out of a commendable passion to restore what they judged to be neglected biblical truths. But this passion, ironically and quickly, resulted in separation and isolation, and a myopic narrowing of Christian truth. Their long-standing claim to be the sole repository of True Faith now appears not only untenable to more and more people but also sadly/comically quaint.

Needed now is training in being more functionally Trinitarian—training which happens best in worship. Along this path lies the way back from isolation to what C. S. Lewis called "mere Christianity"—the great path of Christian orthodoxy transcending denominational traditions and provincial, often esoteric, sectarian claims. But lacking a liturgy and confessional tools in which Trinitarian exercises are embedded, Churches of Christ do not find this training readily at hand. Indeed, strong non- or anti-Trinitarian impulses remain at work.[4] About the only place Trinitarian language regularly appears in most Churches of Christ is in the baptismal formula drawn from Matthew 28:19 ("baptizing them in the name of the Father and of the Son and of the Holy Spirit")—though congregations may go for months without a public baptism. Some congregations occasionally sing the Doxology but, in our experience and observation, its use is not widespread or common.

N. T. Wright suggests a simple exercise for the rebuilding of Trinitarian consciousness. Drawing upon both the Jewish and Eastern Orthodox traditions of daily prayer (the *Shema* and the Jesus Prayer),

Wright commends a simple Trinitarian prayer for use in congregational worship and private devotion:

> Father almighty, maker of heaven and earth:
> > Set up your kingdom in our midst.
> Lord Jesus Christ, Son of the Living God:
> > Have mercy on me, a sinner.
> Holy Spirit, breath of the living God:
> > Renew me (us) and all the world.

For congregational use, it could become a litany, with a leader praying the first line of a stanza and the congregation responding with
the second line. Since the three stanzas cover the basic things a
church should be praying for, they could be used as a framework for
a season of congregational prayer, repeating each phrase periodically
to give balance and rhythm. The three stanzas could also be trans-
posed from petition into praise and confession.

For private daily use, Wright suggests that the words of the
prayer be repeated mentally in the rhythm of one's breathing, inhal-
ing with the first clause of each couplet and exhaling with the second clause. This suggestion may seem strange at first. But if, with
Genesis, we regard breath as part of the gift of God's own life to us
(Gen. 2:2; cf. Acts 17:25), then such a habit of prayer builds on that
truth to become a channel of God's life or breath to us. "Just as
God's breath becomes our breath, so the prayer that has invoked the
living God becomes...part of the constant, loving, and joyful prayer
of the Trinity, and our own prayer."[5] We "inhale," as it were, the
truth and life of God—"Father almighty, maker of heaven and earth";
we "exhale" the breath, the life, that quickens our own lives—"set
up your kingdom in our midst."

This prayer is only one example of the kind of training exercises
we need. There are many other possibilities—whether drawn from
the rich resources of the classic Christian liturgies or inspired by the
fresh new understandings of Trinitarian Life emerging today. The
basic point is that, in our worship, we need explicit exercises to instill

in us a fuller consciousness of the relational nature of our God—the wonderful vision that God's own Life embodies the kind of love in relationship that we long for in our deepest longings.

3. Walking in the disciplines of Trinitarian Spirituality.

A balanced and fulsome Spirituality must be Trinitarian in its focus, that is, modeled after the functions of Father, Son and Spirit.[6] Yet much Christian Spirituality, in practice, becomes structured around one dominant Person of the Trinity: A focus on the Father affirms the value of creation, our common humanity, and a strong emphasis on the physical as a door into or channel of the Spiritual. It brings a sense of being at home in the world and, with it, an appreciation for the arts, for beauty. It instills the principles of order and stability, often leaving little room for the unpredictable and surprising; and it is easily perceived as emotionally cold and aloof.

A focus on the Son stresses the necessity of a personal conversion to and a disciplined following of Jesus Christ. The way of Jesus and the way of the world become very distinct and separate. In popular evangelicalism the focus easily becomes individualistic and subjective, a kind of me-and-Jesus-alone emphasis that tends to make the Body of Christ secondary or even dispensable; and the goodness of creation is easily diminished, so that the church is turned into a withdrawn community.

A focus on the Spirit, as often seen in pentecostal-charismatic movements, brings an intensified sense of Divine Presence an super-natural empowerment. It stresses deep intimacy with God, mighty manifestations of Divine power and the unpredictability of life in the Spirit. But such focus, because it easily creates the expectation that the Christian life be a breathless exciting adventure, marked with the extraordinary at every turn, lends itself to the contrived, the artificial and even the delusionary.

A Spirituality focusing mainly on the Father or on the Son or on the Spirit will be imbalanced and problematic. A balanced Spirituality will be marked by (1) a strong sense of the goodness of the Father's creation—and a corresponding engagement with the world; (2)

emphasis on forgiveness and reconciliation with God through His Son—and the preaching of the gospel of grace; and (3) an openness to God's Presence in intimacy and power—and reliance on that power as the church carries out God's mission.

The classical Spiritual disciplines, in their various forms and traditions, have served for centuries as channels for participation in God's Life. These disciplines are sometimes grouped into three main categories:

(a) *Exercises focusing on God and self.* These include what has been called (i) practicing the presence of God (or the prayer of recollection), where one develops the habit of recalling throughout the day that God is present everywhere and especially in one's own soul; (ii) conformity to the will of God, where one seeks to grow in the discipline of obedience and unite one's will to God in love; and (iii) self-examining prayer, a disciplined taking stock of one's Spiritual condition, a practice often aided by a prayer journal.

(b) *Exercises focusing on the Word.* These include (i) memorization of and meditation upon Scripture and (ii) what has been called "spiritual reading," a discipline with a somewhat different focus than much modern Bible study. Henri Nouwen describes the difference: "Instead of taking the words apart, we should bring them together in our innermost being; instead of wondering if we agree or disagree, we should wonder which words are directly spoken to us. Instead of thinking about the words as potential subjects for an interesting dialogue or paper, we should be willing to let them penetrate into the most hidden corners of our hearts....Only then can we really 'hear and understand.'"[7]

(c) *Exercises focusing on the world.* One of these is what has been termed Spiritual friendship—friendship that is cultivated in Christ and in which one can open the heart and receive counsel, guidance and correction. Another is what was classically called "meditation on the creature"—occasional meditations stirred by things ranging from nature's beauty to a season of illness to a spider's web. Creation is seen as a mirror of God and every creature as able to evoke Spiritual perception. As John Calvin put it, "Wherever you cast your eyes, there is no spot in the universe wherein you cannot discern at least some spark of his glory." According to Hugh of St. Victor, such meditation is "a disciplined contemplation of some creature in order that grace may guide us to see deeply into its message and purpose in the mind of God."[8]

When carefully chosen and shaped into a personal "rule of life," these disciplines can become for us avenues of Trinitarian Life.

4. Finding venues for self-sacrifice.

Dostoyevsky tells the story of a woman who visits a wise and venerable bishop, complaining of a deficiency in her faith, an erosion in her belief in God that seems to increase with age. To paraphrase: "If," she laments, "I could only believe as I did when I was a child everything would be fine. Could you prove it for me? If I had more evidence then I know I could recover my faith and the world would once again become bright and inviting." Most of us can identify with the woman. Because modernity has distanced us from God, we seldom experience Him in ways that regenerate our faith. Often this burden seems too great for our faith and we yearn for something more concrete.

But Dostoyevsky's story continues. After the woman begs the bishop for some tangible proof of God's existence, the bishop responds in a surprising way: "it cannot be proven, but you can be sure of it. The more you progress in acts of love, the greater your faith will become, and the more real God will be to you. This has been tried; this is certain."

The immense pressure placed upon our faith by the modern worldview is not alleviated by proofs but through acts of self-sacrifice. Among other things, Trinitarian Life teaches us that when we act like God we are becoming like God because it is in fact He who is working in us. As a by-product of this we draw closer to Him, we become more sure of Him, and thus our faith is fortified. Our small self-sacrifices identify us with His supreme self-sacrifice. In the strange logic of Trinitarian Life, crises of faith are healed most readily, not in the classroom or through introspection, but by small and large acts of sacrifice—volunteering at a hospital, working with disabled children or surprising an elderly widow by mowing her lawn before she can ask for help.

5. A recovery of mission as our "reason for being."

The triumph of God appears now in the triumphal procession of his people through history. More simply, history goes on because God's Life needs spreading to every corner of the globe and every corner of the human heart. If we understand ourselves as living in the age where "good news" means, among other things, that God's Life is healing the ruptures modern people experience at every turn, then getting that news out must be seen as urgent. More than that, human history continues because God is graciously giving us time to spread this news. As beneficiaries of this good news, the people of God must recover God's mission as their reason for being.

6. Recovering a sense of the world as God's own creation.

The Trinitarian understanding of God demonstrates that God is inextricably related to creation. Among the many things this truth implies is the fact that even the creative work of non-believers is but pro-creation with God. As such, viewed through the eyes of faith, we can detect emanations of God's grace and meaning to us. We see God's traces in political movements, in philosophy, in art, in pop-culture and in every other sphere of human activity. In locating and describing these traces, in hearing and articulating God's whisper to us through these channels, we begin to recover a sense of the world as God's own creation.

Christian teachers and preachers sometimes appeal to movies or popular music to illustrate, in a way that seizes the attention of their audience, some biblical point. This common practice implies something much greater than many of us may realize: because human beings are made in the image of God, when they create (a movie or a song for example) something of God's meaning is transmitted. That meaning is often concealed and will always be distorted, but nonetheless God's meaning is found everywhere in the creations of His creatures.

Certainly we should be wary of many cultural influences, but we should also seek God out in culture even where He seems absent. Calling ourselves "Trinitarian" is a bold, often provocative affirmation that every part of our world is flowing into the unity of God's Life and love. One way of highlighting this dynamic is to recollect His scattered images upon the face of our present culture, recapturing the meaning that only becomes clear and meaningful for those with the faith to see it. Hence going to a concert, an art gallery or even taking in a movie can be more than recreation; it can also be an attentive listening to the echoes of God's truth that resound from creation itself.

7. Praying for the breath or Spirit of God to fill us.
Finally, faced with the vast brokenness and disarray of late modern culture, with the crisis of the postmodern reaction against modernity, with the Spiritual thinness of our own tradition, and the inward focus of many congregations, we must pray for the renewing of God's breath upon us. As Ezekiel was commanded to call for the wind that would come and quicken the dry bones ("Come from the four winds, O breath, and breathe into these slain, that they may live," Ezek. 37:9), so we must call for the Spirit who alone can bring life. To pray such a prayer is to pray for the flowing of those streams of living, healing water promised by Jesus and opened on Pentecost (John 7:38). It is, in effect, to pray that the whole creation may be healed, renewed and begin experiencing the full and true life for which it was created.

Trust, Expectancy and Vision
The good news is that the responsibility for "achieving" Trinitarian Life rests in God and not us; the bad news is exactly the same thing. This calls us to something more challenging than philosophy and more urgent than tomorrow's to-do list, yet it also calls us ultimately into something more rewarding than either. If our description of Trinitarian Life is indeed biblical and alluring then we are called into a posture of radical trust, patient expectancy and faithful awareness

In trust we are open to God's inbreaking Kingdom in this life, in expectancy we shape our lives for that inbreaking, and in awareness we search our lives, churches and world for its signs.

In this posture we are not circumventing the difficult questions (post)modernity poses to us or avoiding the demands for relevance, but taking them both head-on in the conviction that our struggle with (post)modernity is, as Paul says, a spiritual struggle against spiritual forces (Eph. 5:10-17). If the spirits of modernity are to be exorcised from our lives and worship, than we must engage God Spiritually, with head, heart and every other conceivable dimension of our lives. God, who comes to us as God Who Is Spirit, is faithful and will restore wholeness to our broken, splintered and isolated condition.

The challenge is actually very simple and very radical. Our culture is on the precipice of a rebirth or a collapse, and our tradition, inasmuch as it has drunk deeply from the spiritual forces of this culture, stands alongside our culture on that precipice. The lines of certainty drawn in the sand of the modern era turn out to be fault-lines, and the ground, once seemingly firm and secure, is indeed shaking. The most proper response is not trying to find certainty where none exists but to find peace (wholeness) in the arms of our faithful, unshakable Father. How exactly this can be done cannot be prescribed, except to say, at the very least, we are called, even now, into faith, repentance and supplication.

The challenge before us is not simply to affirm the classic Christian doctrine of the Trinity, but to believe it—to act as if it is true. "The advantage of believing in the Trinity," Dallas Willard tells us finally,

> is that we then live as if the Trinity is real: as if the cosmos environing us actually is, beyond all else, a self-sufficing community of unspeakably magnificent personal beings of boundless love, knowledge, and power. And, thus believing, our lives naturally integrate themselves, through our actions, into the reality of such a universe....In faith we rest ourselves upon the reality of the Trinity in action—and it graciously

meets us. For it is there. And our lives are then enmeshed in the true world of God.[9]

In this tumultuous time, when people on every hand are emerging out of a secular worldview and openly hungering for God, nothing could more invigorate and hearten Christians in their mission than this vision—the biblical vision of the Father, His Son, and the Spirit freely sharing their rich Life and perfect Love with us in ways that lead us into true selfhood, satisfying our deepest and most ardent longings for true communion.

Notes

1. For one professor's wrestling with this problem, see Ray Anderson, *Ministry on the Fireline: A Practical Theology for an Empowered Church* (Downers Grove, IL: InterVarsity, 1993), 197-209.

2. C. S. Lewis, *The Weight of Glory and Other Essays* (Grand Rapids, MI: Eerdmans, 1965), 2.

3. For an excellent discussion of learning to find joy and pleasure in God, see John Piper, *Desiring God* (Portland, OR: Multnomah, 1986), 61-87.

4. One example can be seen in some voices insisting that the Spirit should not be worshipped—that praise and adoration should not be addressed to the Father, Son and Spirit, but only to the Father and the Son. In this view songs like "Father, We Love You," where in the third stanza one sings "Spirit, we love you," are inappropriate—and even the classic Doxology ("praise Father, Son and Holy Ghost") becomes suspect. In contrast, the Nicene Creed affirmed that "along with the Father and the Son, the Holy Spirit is to be worshipped and glorified," and the weight of Christian tradition has affirmed this position. For recent broadly ecumenical reaffirmations, see *The Forgotten Trinity* (London: British Council of Churches, 1989-91), and James B. Torrance, *Worship, Community and the Triune God of Grace* (Downers Grove, IL: InterVarsity, 1996), 35-37.

5. N. T. Wright, "The Prayer of the Trinity," in *Bringing the Church to the World: Renewing the Church to Confront the Paganism Entrenched in Western Culture* (Minneapolis, MN: Bethany House, 1992), 209-215. Clark Pinnock explains how a

Trinitarian understanding reframes the practice of prayer: "Prayer is joining an already occurring conversation. The Spirit calls us to participate in the relationship of intimacy between Father and Son and to be caught up in the dance already begun. In prayer on this earth we join the dance and begin to experience the movement and interplay of the trinitarian Persons." *Flame of Love: A Theology of the Holy Spirit* (Downers Grove, IL: InterVarsity, 1996), 46.

6. See Simon Chan, *Spiritual Theology: A Systematic Study of the Christian Life* (Downers Grove, IL: InterVarsity, 1998), 40-56.

7. Henri Nouwen, *Reaching Out: The Three Movements of the Spiritual Life* (London: Fount, 1980), 124.

8. John Calvin, *Institutes of the Christian Religion* 1.5.1; Martin Thornton, *English Spirituality: An Outline of Ascetical Theology according to the English Pastoral Tradition* (London: SPCK, 1963), 112.

9. Dallas Willard, *The Divine Conspiracy: Rediscovering Our Hidden Life in God* (San Francisco, CA: HarperSanFrancisco, 1998), 318.

Index

About the Authors

C. LEONARD ALLEN is the author of *The Cruciform Church: Becoming a Cross-Shaped People in a Secular World* (1990), *Distant Voices: Discovering a Forgotten Past for a Changing Church* (1993), *Things Unseen: How the Theology of Churches of Christ Brought Success in the Modern Era (and Why after Modernity It probably Won't)* (2001), and other books. His writings have been translated into Portugese, Korean and Japanese. He holds the Ph.D. in Christian Thought from the University of Iowa, and has lectured widely as well as conducted seminars for missionaries in various parts of the world. He is married and the father of three children.

DANNY GRAY SWICK is a Ph.D. candidate in Systematic Philosophy at the Institute for Christian Studies, Toronto, Canada. His M.A. thesis was entitled "The Trinitarian Church: The Believers' Church as the Locus of Christian Orthodoxy" (1998). He has served as a Christian educator and ministered with several churches in Texas. He serves as part-time youth minister at the Southern Hills Church of Christ in Buda, Texas.